BUSINESS MANAGEMENT BASICS

BUSINESS
MANAGEMENT
BASICS

CHARLES R WHITLOCK   R DWANE KRUMME
DONALD P CRIVELLONE

KOGAN
PAGE

Copyright © Princeton Press Publications 1987

All rights reserved. No part of this book may be
reproduced or transmitted in any form or by any
means now known or to be invented, electronic or
mechanical, including photocopying, recording, or
by any information storage or retrieval system, without
written permission from the author or publisher,
except for the brief inclusion of quotations in a review.

First published in the United States of America in 1987
entitled *Just Do It* by Princeton Press Publications,
2899 Agoura Road, Box 316, Westlake Village, CA 91361, USA

This edition first published in Great Britain in 1991
by Kogan Page Ltd, 120 Pentonville Road, London N1 9JN

Reprinted 1991

British Library Cataloguing in Publication Data

A CIP record for this book is available from the British Library.
ISBN 0–7494–0468–X

Printed and bound in Great Britain by
Biddles Ltd, Guildford and King's Lynn

To our friend, without whose efforts
this book would not have been possible.

JOHN Y HESS, MD

Contents

Foreword	9
Introduction	11
1. Market-Place	13
2. The Management Wheel	17
3. Profit	19
4. Mission	25
5. Productivity	29
6. Social Responsibility	33
7. Leadership	39
8. Planning	47
9. Goal-Setting	53
10. Organisational Structure	59
11. Communication	67
12. Motivation	71
13. Decision-Making	77
14. Politics	81
15. Data Management	87
16. Product Management	91
17. People	105
18. Delivery Systems	109
19. Other Resources	113
Summary	117
Further Reading from Kogan Page	121

Foreword

This could be the most significant book you'll ever possess. This book is concerned with theories and ideas about growth, development, and the realising of human potential. The authors have drawn from many years of management experience. The ideas presented in this book have been used – and validated – by thousands of people.

The ideas shared with you are ultimately meaningless unless and until you put them into practice, develop your management skills and realise your full potential. Consciously and systematically apply these newly found ideas to your daily activities, and concentrate that activity on specific, clear, measurable goals. This book will help you to convert your dreams, aspirations, ideas and impulses into goal-directed action.

Dr Krumme began his career in marketing, and 17 years later was the Chief Executive Officer of a 1500 employee banking organisation.

Donald Crivellone began his career in front line management positions and serves as President of a bank today. He has managed over 8000 employees in some assignments.

There are times in all our lives which are junctures or turning points. Stop and reflect on where you've been, where you are now and where you are going. Examine your circumstances and pursue a course of action after this self-examination. In your own experience, you have doubtlessly observed an individual who suddenly takes off in pursuit of a challenging goal. You feel his contagious enthusiasm, his zest for living, his boundless energy and his sense of purpose and direction.

Why can't you be that individual soaring to new heights? What is that 'elusive key'? When you purchased this book, you bought the answer. We have given you the tools you will need to become an extremely effective manager. You are responsible for adding the enthusiasm factor. Just do it.

Charles R Whitlock

Introduction

This book is primarily for those who want, or need, a management overview. Perhaps a newly appointed manager. Or someone who soon expects to enter the ranks of management. Or even someone who's been at it for a while but wants to brush up. Our purpose is to help you understand some fundamental management concepts. The concepts are straightforward and can be read through reasonably quickly. We provide the foundation for you to build on. Your understanding of what is presented here, however, will be enhanced if you *observe* how the concepts are applied by managers you know. Discuss these concepts with others. Ask one of the experienced managers you know to answer your questions.

The model or device we use is called the Management Wheel. It provides a handy way to depict key relationships that management orchestrates in running the company. It also suggests the *balance* necessary for the company to run smoothly: balance among the jobs to be done, the management skills needed to function well and the resources to be employed.

The most important relationship for you to keep in mind is that between you and your company. Your 'company' refers to your boss, your colleagues, and the people who work for you. All are important. All of you together constitute a team which competes for the prize in the market-place. You score every time someone buys your product or service. Everyone in the company has something to do with the score. As a manager, you are responsible for the performance of part of the team. The quality of your performance is established by those who work for you. Your job, for the most part, is to get things done *through people*, the people assigned to you.

You will find it fairly easy to understand the concepts

in the Management Wheel. But understanding management concepts and *being* a manager are different. Although the basics apply to all management jobs, the specific circumstances vary. Companies are different, and so are their opportunities and problems. Bosses are different, and so are their expectations. Management positions are different up and down the organisation, and so is the complexity of the jobs to be done. People are different, and so are their abilities to get the job done. Your management task is to apply the basics to your particular circumstances so that you can manage effectively a part of the company process. You can read books and observe others – you had better do both. But the applications of the concepts you learn are yours to make. 'Management' really comes back to you. You and your boss. You and your colleagues. You and your staff. You and your company. Simply stated, you must do it.

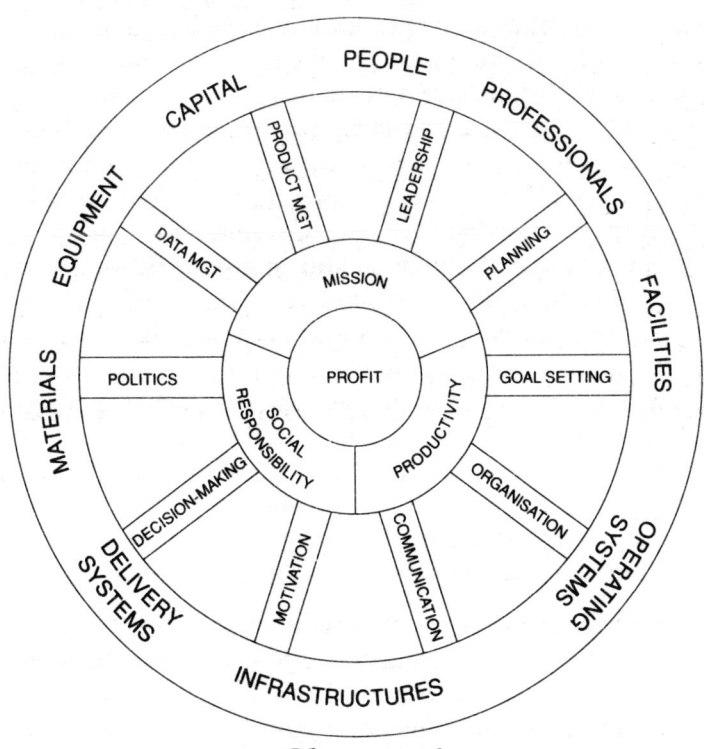

Chapter 1
Market–Place

The market-place is the arena where every business enterprise is finally judged winner or loser. It is the arena for the exchange of products or services with customers. It is where you and your competitors meet head on to convince the buyer – the customer – to choose you rather than the competition. Whether you manage a retail shop or a production line, your efforts will finally be judged as successful or unsuccessful in the market-place. Every manager, then, must understand how his or her

Business Management Basics

area of responsibility helps the company to compete in the market arena.

Companies do not make mistakes. People make mistakes. Too many mistakes, of course, can cause lasting damage – even failure – in the market-place. For the market-place is also made up of people. People have perceptions, make judgements, have memories. Companies can face years of expensive rebuilding for mistakes that have been widely publicised. In some cases, companies pay for the actions of others, actions completely beyond their immediate control. Consider, for example, the outspoken claims of junior health minister, Edwina Currie, about the salmonella contamination of eggs and chickens in the late Eighties. Fear in the market virtually drove a product out. Companies with reputations for poor service or quality run much greater risks than companies that charge more for products or service. People are prepared to pay more for better quality. When the salmonella – free egg stamp was introduced, the eggs bearing it commanded a higher price.

In making the decision to buy, people take a number of factors into consideration. Some of the more noteworthy are:

- **Need** for the product or service. A car must be replaced when worn out, a product need. A car must be repaired when broken, a service need.
- **Desire** for the product or service. Some things people simply want, as opposed to need. Eating is a need, but going to a restaurant for dinner is a desire. When a specific restaurant is selected, the 'buying decision' has been made.
- **Price.** Assuming a comparable level of quality, people will generally look for a lower price. Companies charging higher prices than their competitors must convince potential buyers that the product is superior in terms of quality, features, and perceived value to the buyer.
- **Quality.** People generally expect more when they pay more. However, though difficult to define precisely, people have some minimum expectation of value when they buy anything. An inexpensive pen that runs out frequently does not meet the minimum expectation of

value. Nor does a rude cashier in a bank. The forms and levels of quality differ widely, but each buying decision brings with it a minimum expectation of value.
- **Convenience.** This term also takes many forms. For example, convenience may be how close the supermarket is to home. Or it may be a weekend plumbing service. Long queues may make another bank or grocery shop more convenient even though the customer may have to drive or walk a few minutes longer to get there.

  Convenience can be influenced by need. Patients obviously undergo greater inconvenience to see the consultant of their choice than the same people will accept when they decide where to have their clothes dry-cleaned.

  Desire influences the buyer's view of convenience. A boating enthusiast may pass several boat dealers to buy a specific product.

  Price often influences the value buyers associate with convenience. The growth of cash and carry outlets in recent years demonstrates buyer willingness to drive farther and queue longer to save money.
- **Risk.** If the potential buyer believes that the risk is too high, the purchase will not be made. Consider, for example, the reluctance of tourists to travel to Northern Ireland or to the Basque country in northern Spain when the threat of terrorism is highly publicised. Regardless of the price, quality or real value offered, many people will not buy. When there is a perceived risk of bank failure, depositors take their money elsewhere. Those threatened with unemployment frequently alter their buying habits dramatically. Or risk may simply take the form that the bread is stale or the film isn't worth seeing.

These and other dynamics are constantly at work in the market-place. People differ, and so do their attitudes concerning needs for products and services. Circumstances differ, altering the buying decisions people make. You will be a better manager if you understand the nature of the market-place your company serves. Every member of the management team either helps or hinders the company – there is no neutral ground. The

Business Management Basics

overstaffed accounts department drives up overheads, making competitive pricing that much more difficult when potential buyers are most sensitive to price. The personnel department with ineffective screening places the wrong people in customer service, resulting in unhappy employees and customers. Each management function has something to do with the relationship between the company and the market-place (or the function should not exist in the company).

If your management responsibilities do not involve direct contact with customers, don't excuse yourself and leave understanding of the market-place to someone else. Somehow, somewhere in the process, what you do will have a bearing upon the decision to buy. Part of your responsibility as a manager is to understand how and where your actions influence that decision.

The following chapters deal with the major management concerns of the business. But all these concerns are futile if they do not enable your company to convince potential buyers to choose your product or service. Know who your potential buyers are, why they should buy from you, and how your management role helps to influence favourably the ultimate decision to buy. When you decide to become a member of management, you accept the responsibility of helping your company to win in the market-place. There is no other arena, and there is no desirable alternative to winning.

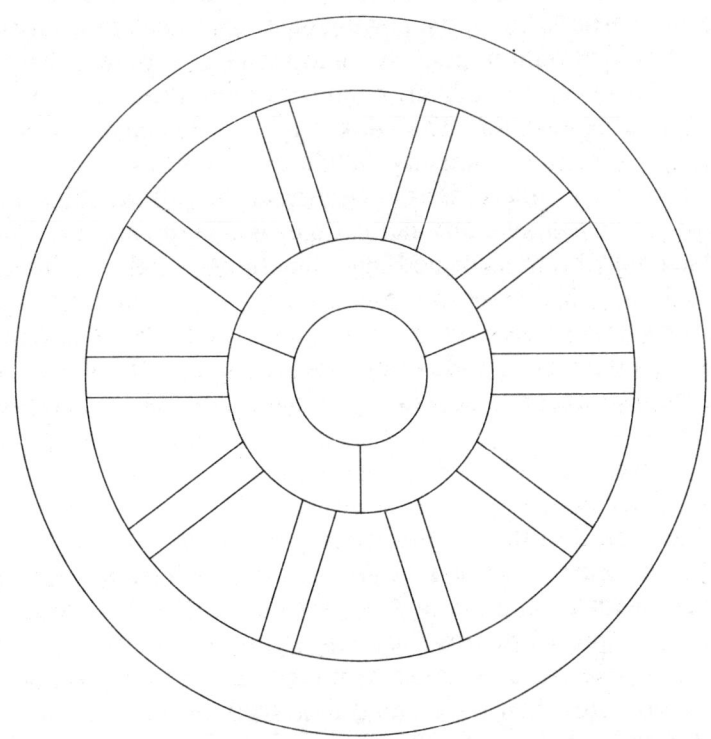

Chapter 2
The Management Wheel

The Management Wheel graphically depicts the major elements in the business process. Understanding these elements, what they are and how they relate to each other, is the intellectual focus of management. Keeping these elements in balanced relationship with each other is the job of management. Getting the job done through people is the essence of management.

Let's look briefly at the elements of the Management Wheel. At its hub are Profits, the goal of the enterprise. If the hub

Business Management Basics

disintegrates, if the company is not profitable, the wheel comes to a screeching halt. Surrounding the hub are three fundamental organisational tasks: Mission, Productivity and Social Responsibility. Management must articulate a mission for the organisation, assemble and manage resources that are Productively employed, and conduct the enterprise in a Socially Responsible manner. The spokes are the management skills needed to run the company. While the emphasis on a specific skill will vary under different circumstances, all the skills must exist within the company all the time. At the rim are resources, which must be transformed into something of value to be sold at a profit. The resources presented here are common to all businesses. For instance, service industries use less equipment than manufacturing industries. But both types of industry use all the resources depicted in the Management Wheel to varying degrees.

The wheel as an image suggests balance, motion and direction. But the image is at best abstract. The reality of business is discovered in the application of the abstract: as the saying goes, the real test is when the tyre hits the road. People working together for a common purpose create balance. People doing their jobs propel the organisation. People direct the company on its course. As a manager, you serve and lead others. To do well, you must first understand that every business process is, in the final analysis, a people process. It is as good or bad as the people who carry out the process. The Management Wheel revolves around business concepts. Business revolves around people – buyers and sellers, managers and workers. You want to be a better manager? Understand the concepts and their interrelationships. Apply them in your relationships with the boss and the subordinate. Remember that your application is where the tyre of the Management Wheel hits the road.

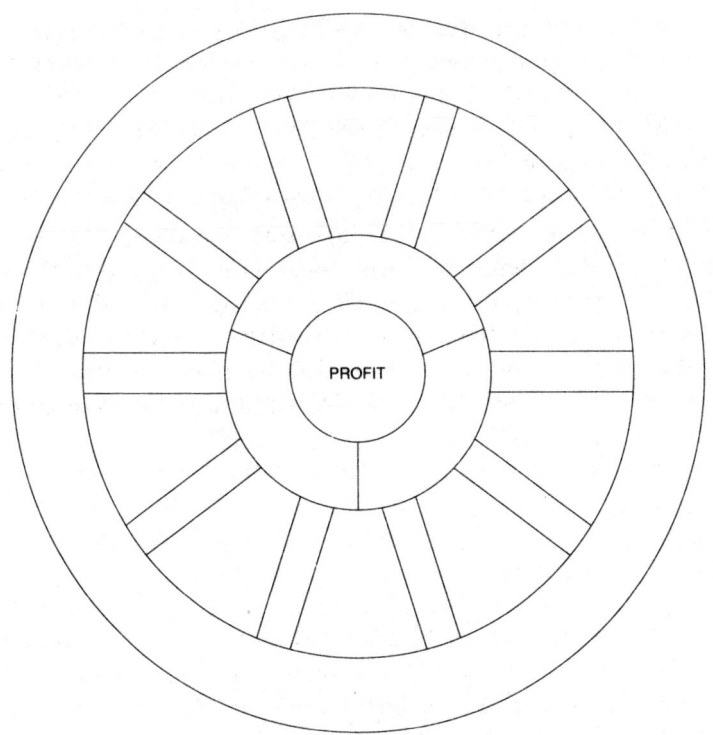

Chapter 3
Profit

(The goal of business)

Unless specifically set up as a non-profit-making organisation, the goal of every business is to generate profits. The term 'profit', however, has no measurable value if it is only talked about, bantered about or even complained about. Though profit can be finitely stated as a goal and precisely measured as a result, profit can elude management's efforts. Profitability, it

Business Management Basics

seems, inevitably eludes companies whose management reveres it only at annual corporate revivals, called shareholders' meetings.

The level of profitability a company *should* achieve can be decided by management somewhat objectively. Analytical tools are readily available to help set profit goals. The level of profitability a company *does* achieve, on the other hand, is more subjectively determined. Workers have varying levels of skill and motivation, which determine, for the most part, the level of productivity. Managers have varying degrees of ability to deal with workers' skill and motivation levels, which determine, for the most part, the level of company performance. The best case, of course, is one in which the company does achieve what it should achieve: workers know how to do their jobs and are dedicated to their tasks; managers match the jobs to be done with the people to get them done, and direct the work process to the desired conclusion.

Attitude – of the worker and the manager – is the single most important influence on company profitability. The proper view of profit is that it brings:

- Continuance of the enterprise
- Growth of the company
- Security for employees and shareholders
- Capacity for research
- Opportunity for improved social well-being.

The proper attitude towards profit is that: 'Making a profit is my responsibility too.'

You, the manager, play the key role in shaping the attitudes of your workers. Start with your own attitude. 'Profit is somebody else's responsibility.' Does this statement describe your attitude? It is easy to say no to the question, but it is important not to answer too quickly. Be honest about it. The people who work for you mirror your attitude. They will be honest about it in the kind of work they do for you – and for your company. Holding the proper view of profit is easy if you have only memorised the words for use at management meetings, staff motivation sessions and the like. Displaying the proper attitude towards your company's profit performance is

Profit

hard work. You have to understand how you and your staff affect profit performance. Then you have to care enough to make concern for profit your responsibility too. Answering a few questions will help you to concentrate on the attitude you bring to the profit issue.

- Do you feel good, sometimes boast a little, about the number of people under you? (If so, you may in fact be contributing more to your ego than to your company's profit performance.)
- Do you wish your office could be larger? (If so, you may run the risk of expanding your corporate territory at some cost to your company's profitability – most companies cannot afford to support internal territorial expansion.)
- Do you know what your company's profit goal is for this year? How does the actual performance year-to-date compare to plan? How does your area of management responsibility directly and/or indirectly impact the bottom line of your company?

A profitable use of your time will be to add to this list. Include such questions as how you spend your time and your company's money, the level of understanding among members of your staff concerning the company's profit performance, and whose responsibility it is to make a profit this year.

Organisational Tasks

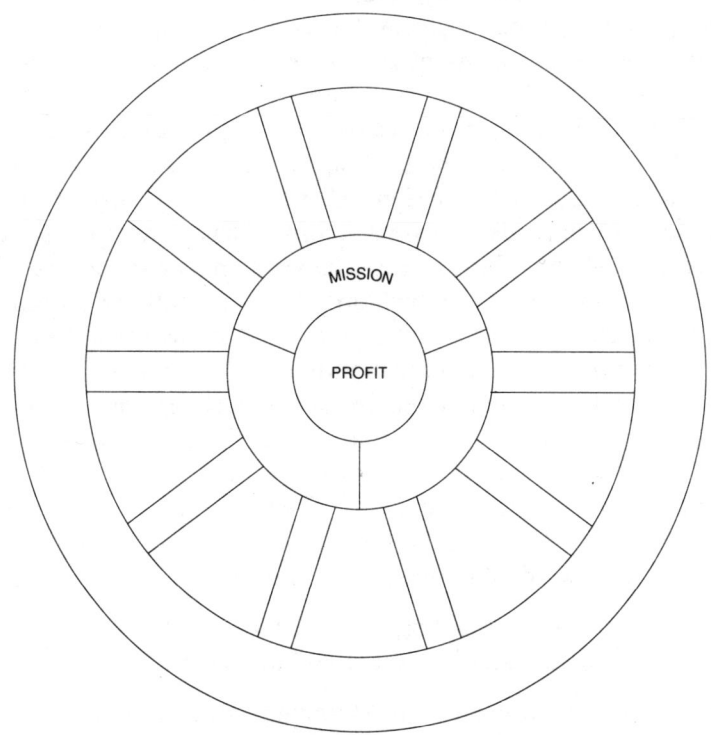

Chapter 4
Mission

(An organisational task)

The statement of mission is analogous to the flight plan submitted by a pilot to set out the destination, the course to be followed and the estimated time of arrival. Without a flight plan, the situation that comes to mind is the one when the pilot speaks to the passengers over the public address system: 'Ladies and Gentlemen: This is your pilot speaking. I have good news and bad news. The bad news is that we're hopelessly lost. The good news is that we're making good time!'

The mission statement of the company is in fact the vision and purpose of the organisation. It is the general framework within which management tests its key decisions. The mission determines the direction the company will take in its strategic actions – moving us from where we are to where we want to be. The roots of the organisation's culture can be traced back to the statement of mission. Consciously or unconsciously, formally or informally, every company has a mission. It may exist only in the minds of top management, in which case the risk is that the actions of lower management staff are disjointed and inconsistent, lacking the 'glue' that holds managers to a common purpose. The understanding of the company's mission creates motion in management and underlines consistency of action and direction. Every manager in the company needs to understand the statement of mission, understand where they are taking the company and why. Chester Barnard, considered one of the fathers of modern scholarship and management theory, makes this statement about mission:

> The inculcation of belief in the real existence of a common purpose is an essential executive function.[1]

That 'common purpose' is the statement of mission: it describes the *fundamental values* of the company – why it exists, the markets it seeks to serve, and how it will serve the markets selected. These are the values that management and staff have to understand and buy into. It is important to bear in mind that management and staff are people, all of whom act and react according to the value set they have adopted. The mission statement helps to bring a coherence to individual values as they pertain to the individual's role at work.

The better mission statement, as it applies to you (the manager), has the following characteristics:

- It is simply stated and easily understood.
- It makes sense, in terms of products delivered or services rendered; that is, the mission applies to the nature of the business – manufacturing or retailing, for example –

Mission

and the markets served. You can quickly appreciate the absurdity of a mission statement for a large aerospace manufacturer that calls for selling products to small retailers.
- It is widely communicated within the company. It is included in new-employee orientation, in employee handbooks, and, when circumstances warrant, occasionally discussed with the entire staff.
- It serves as a reference check for major decisions, such as new markets to be entered, new products to be developed and the like.
- It is credible, something you and your staff can believe in.

Creation of a mission statement is an *event*. It takes place at a point in time, presumably at the inception of the company. But efforts precede the creation of a mission. These efforts are to understand the external environment in which the company will operate (economic conditions, regulatory and legislative issues, social attitudes that may have a bearing upon company performance, and so on); the market capacity available for the product or service; what the company is in business for (is a building society, for example, formed to provide mortgages for private home-owners or to provide a deposit facility for savers – or to do both as part of an all-round provision of financial services for the consumer?) Based on an understanding of the environment, the market, and why the company is in operation, the mission statement is created.

While creating a statement of mission is an event, the execution of mission is a *process*. Strategic plans, annual business plans, quarterly goals, all spring from the mission statement and are part of an ongoing series of activities or process. The way people think about customers, about each other, about their bosses, all spring from the mission statement. The actions of people that *become* the company constitute the process of execution of the mission statement.

As manager, you have probably inherited the statement of mission for your company. It may be called by a different name, such as 'corporate purpose'. It may not be in written

Business Management Basics

form, but it manifests itself in the values (internal performance expectations and external concentration upon customers) that top managers adopt. Your responsibility as a manager is to understand the mission of your company and how it applies to your management responsibilities. There is a common purpose for your company. Be sure that your purpose as a manager is consistent with that of your company.

Note

[1] Cited in William R Tolbert, 'Executive Mind, Timely Action', *Revision*, Vol 6, No 1 (Spring 1983), p 6.

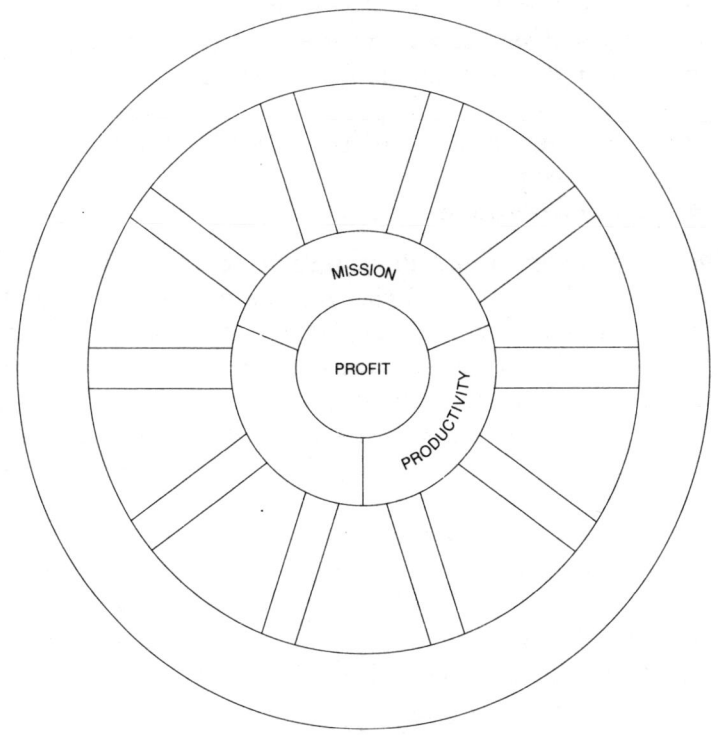

Chapter 5
Productivity

(A management task)

Productivity is one of the most critical issues company managements face today. Several variables affect the level of productivity: equipment, technology, facilities, environment and so on. But the attitudes of people probably have the greatest influence upon any company's productivity levels. Automation and technology can clearly advance productivity. On the other

Business Management Basics

hand, several factors can retard it:

- Declining investment in capital equipment
- Declining research and development
- Abnormal increases in cost (energy, for example)
- Government regulation that requires extra steps in a process
- A changing work force requiring time for the learning curve to be passed
- Lack of innovation.

The last two items listed above involve people, and people do make the difference. Declining motivation was not listed but could be listed several times because it is so important in productivity. Many tasks, many processes can be automated. But the way people feel and what they think about their work cannot. For example, a study of the American motor industry showed that with *twice* the capital investment, American car workers are *30 per cent less productive* than their counterparts in Japan. An article concerning productivity of the Honda of America plant in Ohio, as compared with the Jeep division of American Motors Corporation 100 miles away in Toledo, stated: 'Productivity is more than a number and an economic concept; it is people and machinery – and, most important, attitudes.'[1] The article goes on:

> Productivity is a much-discussed economic term, but it also has a powerful human dimension. Why do some factories run so smoothly, while others writhe in turmoil? Does the physical condition of the plant tell the answer, or is there something more – something about the quality of the people, their orientation towards one another, their bosses and the nature of the work itself? Honda and Jeep have one thing in common: output. Each working day Honda turns out 875 four-wheel passenger vehicles powered by internal combustion engines; Jeep produces 750 of the machines. Beyond that, the similarities end . . . [In contrast to Jeep] what bonds the company [Honda] together and helps generate its growth is a kind of corporate chemistry – an environment that encourages both labour and management

Productivity

at the firm to regard themselves as 'us' rather than as 'us versus them'.[2]

In another comparison, a production line worker for a television manufacturer compared the production process between US ownership and Japanese ownership. 'When I worked for the American company, the television sets came down the conveyor belt continuously. I installed as many parts as I could before it moved down the line – the conveyor belt kept moving. Defects were high. After the Japanese bought us, they installed a pedal. When I need to, I can stop the conveyor belt to finish my job. My television sets now have very few defects, because I know how to do my job, and I have the time to do it the right way.' This worker's attitude and productivity improved simultaneously.

Low productivity causes significant problems for a company. The cost per unit of output goes up. When that happens, higher prices must be charged in the market-place to cover the increase in cost. Otherwise, profitability goes down. Efficient competitors can quickly establish a price advantage in the market because the inefficient company will not be able to absorb a higher level of production cost for very long.

A widening circle of companies has started to think and do something about improving productivity. Those enjoying success have several management emphases in their programmes:

- **Commitment** to improving productivity starts with top management and finds its way down through every organisational level.
- **Definitions** of productivity improvement are communicated in a manner that makes sense to the people who are supposed to become more productive.
- **Goals** established to improve productivity create the need to stretch, but not tear, the organisation.
- **Measurements** are employed to ensure that progress, or lack of it, is being monitored and that what is desired is being achieved.
- **Training** is in itself productive, concentrating on what needs to be taught and to whom.

Business Management Basics

- **Participation** in finding better ways to do the job is extended to everyone on the payroll.
- **Rewards** are given with publicity among the staff, so that those doing a job well are recognised and praised.

We view productivity as a major task because most companies need a lot more of it. Productivity cannot be acquired in the form of a particular expertise, but it can be achieved with the proper investment: thinking, capital spending, managing, working. The most important contribution you, as a manager, can make to your company's overall level of productivity is to ensure that your staff are motivated, that they care about themselves, each other, their jobs and their company.

Notes

[1] *Forbes*, 'A Tale of Two Worlds', (16 June, 1986), p 102.
[2] *Forbes*, pp 102–5.

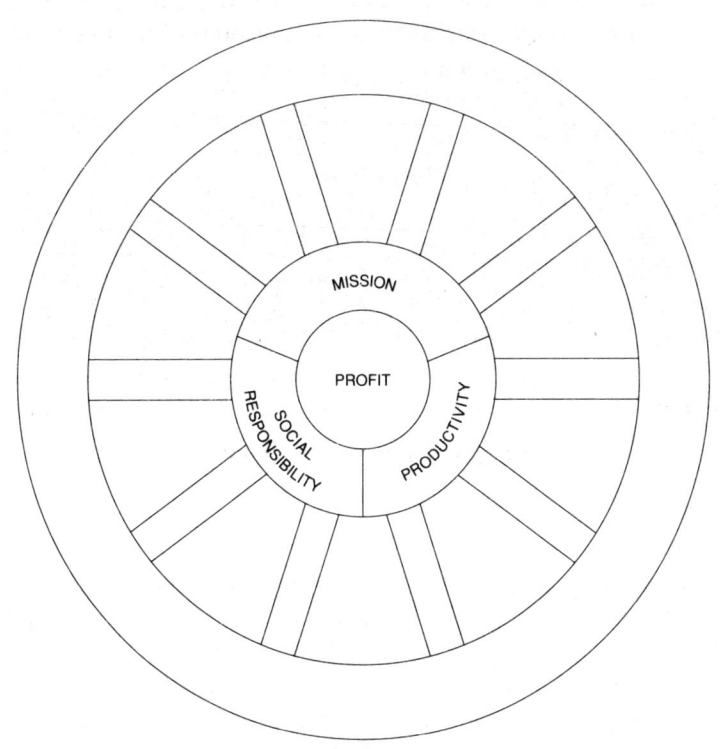

Chapter 6
Social Responsibility

(An organisational task)

The area of social responsibility is considered an organisational task because it requires the formal attention of management in the current environment. The likelihood is that the current situation will continue in the years ahead.

The introduction of limited liability allowed businesses to expand, for which capital was essential. The need for capital became sufficiently acute that smaller individual investors were looked to as an additional source of private market capital. Like any investor, smaller shareholders had a vested interest in company performance. Because interaction between company management and hundreds or thousands of individual shareholders was impossible, boards of directors were formed to allow shareholders to elect representatives to protect their investments from mismanagement. Part of the 'deal' in raising capital from the private market is that management subjects itself to the authority of the board of directors. What is now a routine arrangement was in the early years a noteworthy encroachment upon what had been a virtual management independence. Although the early versions of a board of directors had limited influence (and no personal liability if shareholders were poorly represented), the foundations were placed for a growing influence of outsiders over company management.

Along with the growth of small investors came the emergence of the business analyst whose observations about company performance – past and expected – began to have a measurable effect upon an individual company's ability to raise capital. As a result, management had to pay an increasing amount of attention to analysts. A 'bad review' could drive potential and existing investors away from a company, drying up sources of capital. Therefore, management began to take actions that would gain the favour of analysts, whose influence over management thinking today is widespread and substantial.

Another development that has shown lasting significance was the rise of organised labour. Whereas before management had virtually complete control over labour, the widespread organisation of trade unions shifted power from management to labour. Unions began to have influence over management decisions. The relationship between company management and the work force was changed dramatically.

The media also played a key role in management's actions on issues of social significance. The exploitation of the work force and/or the environment by large corporations was reported nationally and internationally. No longer could management ignore the consequences of publicity that both reflected and shaped social attitudes, legislative activities and political relationships.

What began at a relatively slow pace has accelerated in the last 30 years. Management liability, regulatory liability resulting from legislation, and market liability resulting from consumer protection actions all require substantial commitments of management energy and corporate resources. Managers at many levels today are accountable to many on the outside. Virtually any manager must be capable of purposeful interaction with allies and adversaries outside the company. Believe it or not, you could get a call from the media. You are well-advised to be prepared. Saying nothing in response to questions can be bad, but saying the *wrong* thing can cause lasting damage to your company.

It is not too soon to think about what you and your company are doing in the area of social responsibility. You should be aware of your company's programmes that are designed for community benefit. Being aware is the best defence against the possibility of being caught by surprise if a criticism is levelled. Being involved in community schemes is the best way to find opportunities to be of service to the community. You need to be aware of relevant social issues and, as they pertain to your company, be involved in the process to address them. Constructive community service is an important asset to your company. Responsible service to your community is also valuable service to your company. You should know the social leaders, what their concerns are and what consequences those concerns may have in your company.

Social responsibility will continue to be an important measure of a company's 'value' and management effectiveness. There are many publics to be served. Establishing and maintaining solid relationships with those publics are as much a part of management's job as is the generation of profits for investors. You are a part of management. It is a part of your job too.

Organisational Skills

The chapters in this section deal with the skills that must be present in a company's organisation for the company to function well. If you are experienced in business, you may notice an absence of several functions conventionally included under the heading of organisational skills. These include such areas as finance, marketing, personnel (human resource), public relations, and the like. We define these areas as 'professional' skills. They are unquestionably important to the business process and are acquired by the company to perform specialised functions.

The organisational skills referred to in the Management Wheel are skills that every member of management must possess. The company cannot function well if managers are not skilled in leadership, planning, motivation and decision making, to name a few. Because the skills discussed in the following chapters are important to every manager in the company, we view them as general skills necessary to the entire organisation.

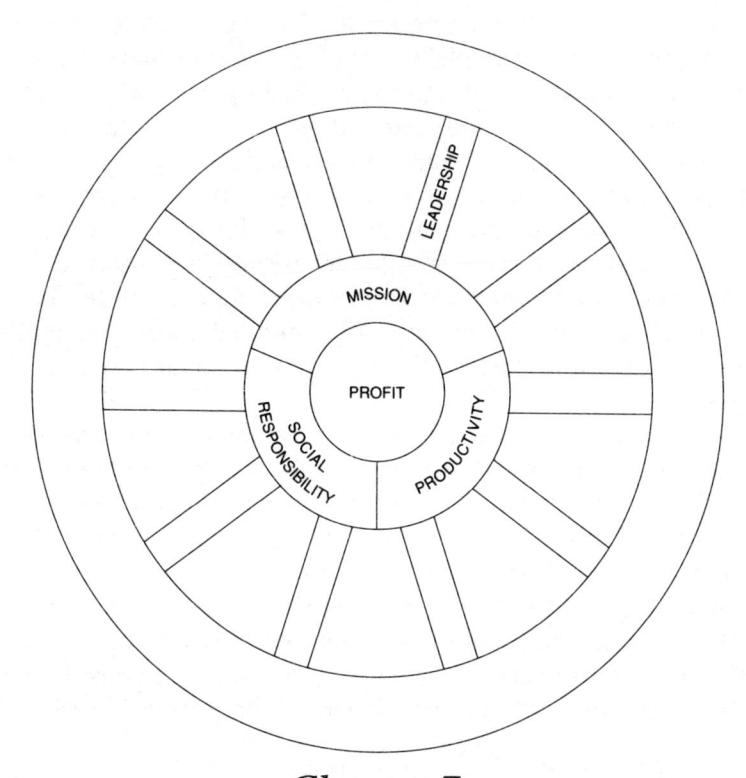

Chapter 7
Leadership

(An organisational skill)

To distinguish yourself as a manager, to perform as well as you can, to have the best chance for upward mobility in the management structure of your company, you must have the qualities of leadership. Of course, there is no single set of characteristics that uniformly applies to everyone, but there are some general characteristics that you can uniquely make

Business Management Basics

your qualities so that you do emerge as a leader in your organisation.

Perhaps the most important attribute of a leader is in the recognition that 'example' sets the pattern for others to follow. Edmund Burke put it this way: 'Example is the school of mankind, and they will learn at no other.'[1] What you say and how you say it, what you do and how you do it, the person that you are in your company role and in your personal role, these become the example you set for others. And more widespread recognition as a leader means less freedom from the responsibilities of leadership: you are watched more closely, listened to more attentively, and imitated more frequently. Wherever you are seen, whenever you are heard, you set the example.

The best leaders use their role as example to bring out better qualities in those who follow them. The best leaders both speak well and listen well. They know when to lead and when to follow. Effective leaders have a strong team with them – any member of the team could be, or in fact *is*, a leader. Leaders have a view of today and a vision of tomorrow. They mould what is from the mass of what can be. They work with and through others to create form from possibility. Leaders share in common a willingness to risk failure in the pursuit of success:

> . . . [the] 'Executive Mind' is fired by a passion to accomplish an improbable purpose and is, consequently, fundamentally optimistic even at the darkest moment of despair. This optimism is in no sense a fatalistic 'just wait, everything will be all right' attitude, but rather the ability to draw energy from a supreme challenge or demand.[2]

If you are drawn to the challenge, are energised by the demands of accomplishing something that at the time seems impossible, then you have experienced the 'calling' of leadership. If you are willing to share in the tribulations of the pursuit and the rewards of accomplishment, then you have the 'attitude' of leadership. If you are doing these things regularly, then you are a leader. As a leader, you then no doubt:

- **Lead by example**

Leadership

- You know that your 'work ethic' will be assumed by others. Work ethic does not merely refer to working hard. It means how you view your company, your customers, your staff, and what you have to do to help your company win in the market-place.
- You practise what you preach.
- You are consistent.
- You are excited about the purpose, about the mission. And stay true to it.
- You recognise that your judgement may be questioned, but that your integrity will not.
- You stay in touch with the staff and customers.
- You delegate, showing trust.

• **Are credible**
- You tell the truth.
- You admit mistakes, and accommodate the mistakes of others.
- You say so when you don't know.
- You select good people.
- You keep promises.
- You encourage innovation, reward success and stand by your staff when they err.

• **Are interesting** because you are interested.

• **Are believed** because you believe.

Sometimes an example is the best way to make the point. This incident actually happened.

A major firm undertook some severe cost-cutting measures including curtailment of perks, establishment of ceilings for salary increases, staff reductions, etc. The firm's executives decided to disperse into group meetings with managers in various regions. The purpose, obviously, was to explain directly the reasons for the dramatic steps being taken. The chairman of the firm went to his first meeting, but arrived a little late. The meeting, none the less, seemed to go well – good interaction, airing of concerns, managers contributing. The meeting concluded, the chairman walked

41

out with several managers. He wished them well, walked to his new Jaguar, and his driver drove him away. One influential manager commented: 'Cut costs. Right! At least he should have taken a taxi for a mile or so before his Jag picked him up. I wonder how that's being paid for.'

As you can appreciate, riding off in the new Jaguar had more impact than all the policy pronouncements and meetings on cost-cutting combined. If you as a leader say one thing and do another, those who follow are most likely to follow your example.

A leader inevitably emerges in every group, large and small. Regardless of your group size, you will influence others and be influenced by them. You have to observe desirable qualities in others and make them yours, provided that you do so naturally.

- Be a good listener, and others will listen to you.
- Understand your company (its purpose, culture, and leaders) so that your perspective adds value to the process.
- Concentrate on service: to your customers, your management, your peers.
- Care about your staff. In serving, you lead.
- Know your circumstances.
- When it is time to speak, speak. When you do speak, say something worth listening to.

I simply know that I smell things, I feel situations, and when the crowd is silent I understand what it silently says. And I say it with a voice, with the proper words.

Lech Walesa[3]

Leadership style

While all leaders share some characteristics, there is no common mould. Style is a matter of individual make-up. It seems too obvious to have to say that one person's style won't fit others. Yet many would-be leaders try to become someone they are not. They try to put on a 'suit' of leadership characteristics

Leadership

that is tailored for someone else. The consequences are obvious to everyone else. The suit does not fit. As a leader, you simply must *be yourself*. You speak the same language, discuss similar issues, wear comparable clothes and share common thought processes with those around you. To distinguish yourself from those around you, use your own desirable personal attributes that single you out. As a leader, you have to be a part of the group and apart from the group.

The pragmatic criterion is: *Does your style work?*

If your boss listens to what you say, you're probably on target. If your interaction with peers is worthwhile and pleasant, you're probably on target. If the feedback you get (words, action, 'body signals') suggests that you're all right, you probably are. If, on the other hand, some of these things are missing, you have some work to do. Find out why your style is not working, even if that means you have to discuss your style with someone whose judgement you have confidence in, and change the way you come across. But be natural about it or the changes will not produce the desired result.

Different styles work for different people. The important point is that the style must work for the individual. Consider, for example, two sports leaders: football managers, Brian Clough of Nottingham Forest and Terry Venables of Tottenham Hotspur. Clough is outspoken, abrupt, says what he thinks. Venables is more affable, chatty, less volatile. Two distinctive styles, yet both men are highly effective as managers and as leaders. The differences are noticeable, but the similarities are noteworthy. Players follow both managers with equal vigour because both have several key qualities in common: they are honest, care about their purpose and their players, reward their players, make winners of their players. Two different styles, but each satisfies the pragmatic criterion: *It works*.

In the business world, there are almost as many attempts to categorise management styles as there are observers and practitioners. Some distinctions that have reappeared frequently are:

Business Management Basics

Autocratic/Dictatorial
It is easy to work out the meaning of this one: it's the 'Don't confuse me with facts, I've made up my mind!' syndrome. This style is directive, order-giving, and has no room for interaction or participation. This is obviously not a good leadership style because others follow out of fear rather than respect.

Laissez-faire/Anything Goes
This style is the opposite of the autocratic. It is not effective because there is no leadership. Everyone is free to do whatever seems appropriate.

Democratic/Participative
Not surprisingly, this is the desirable style. It provides for interaction between the leader/manager and the staff. It allows those who have something worthwhile to say to speak out. It allows members of the staff who have their own leadership qualities to emerge. And it works.

The truth is that all managers have, at least at some point, adopted each of these three styles in their management behaviour at different times and under different circumstances. More important are those qualities which characterise the manager *over time*. The predominant qualities over time determine leadership or management style. The easy convention is to place those you do not like in the 'undesirable' categories and put those you do like, and yourself, in the desirable ones. More purposeful is a sustained effort to listen to what your environment tells you. Your style works in most situations or it doesn't. It's that simple.

If your style is not working, the good news is that you are capable of realising that it isn't. Given that realisation, it is time to do something about it. If you listen to feedback, look at yourself, discard bad characteristics to adopt good ones and lead responsibly, you will satisfy the pragmatic criterion: *It will work*.

Paying attention to interpersonal relationships, understanding your associates, interacting with your boss and listening

Leadership

to your subordinates, are the keys to effective leadership. How you do these things is a matter of leadership style. To be successful, every company needs sound management and strong leadership. As a manager, as a potential or active leader, there is no neutral position. You hinder your company or you help your company to distinguish itself in the market-place.

Notes

[1] Edmund Burke, *On a Regicide Peace*.
[2] William R Tolbert, 'Executive Mind, Timely Action,' *Revision*, Vol 6, No 1 (Spring 1983), pp 6–7.
[3] Cited in Tolbert, p 8.

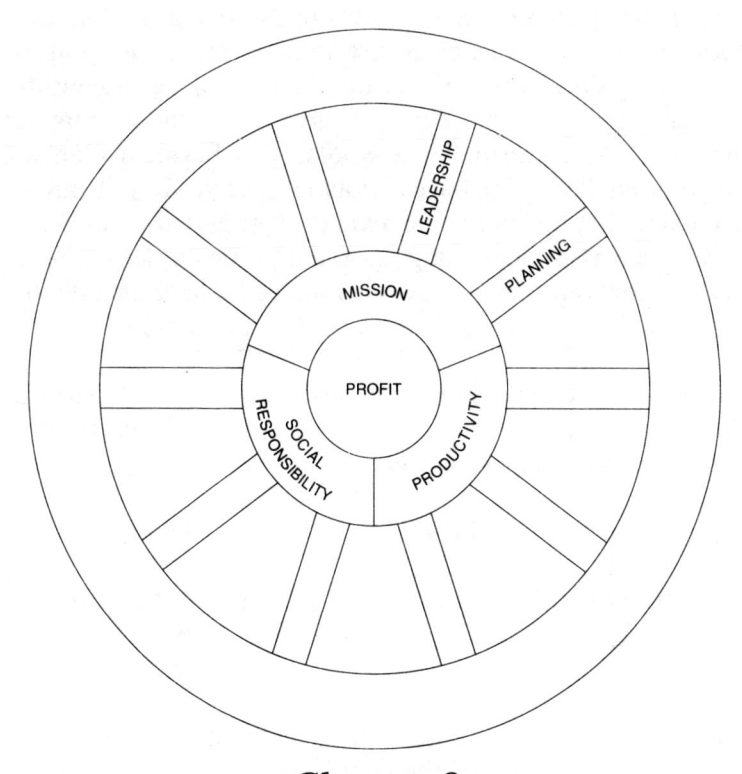

Chapter 8
Planning

(An organisational skill)

In this section, we will review the planning *Process*. Although the creation of a formal written business plan is an event, the activities that lead up to the formal business plan constitute a process. Planning flows from the statement of mission and into the creation of annual business goals, which become part of the annual business plan.

> **Business Plan**
> The mission statement may be only one or two pages long, with enough words to give a clear direction to the organisation. But it is the business plan of the major units of an organisation that develops the more detailed direction of those units, and therefore the company as a whole. The business plan may range from 20 to 30 pages, double spaced. It is from this document that the individual managers prepare their individual unit goals. Also, depending upon the particular structure and size of a company, each major division could have an individual business plan, summing up the total corporate plan.

The diagram below shows the vertical process of planning. The two-way arrows describe the interactive exchange at the individual management levels.

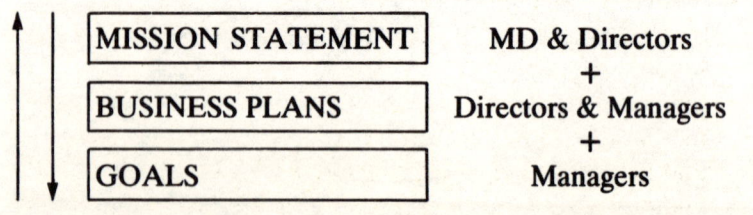

MISSION STATEMENT	MD & Directors
	+
BUSINESS PLANS	Directors & Managers
	+
GOALS	Managers

The mission statement is developed by the managing director, with the participation of the next level of management (those reporting directly to the MD). Also, the board of directors must support the mission statement.

The business plan is developed by those reporting to the MD, with the participation of managers reporting directly to the MD's managers.

Goals are set by the individual functional units (division or department managers, depending upon the organisational structure). The diagram above assumes only three management levels in the company. The application of the planning process, of course, will depend upon the actual structure of the company.

Although application of the planning process must be specific to each company, there are some general observations that apply to every company:

Planning

- As mentioned, planning is not an event. It is in fact a process. Too many companies make it an annual punishment.
- Planning consists of a blend of short-term and long-term considerations. The 'either/or' syndrome is to be avoided: today's actions must sustain the enterprise in the short term and lead to improved overall performance in the long term.
- Planning does not begin afresh each year. Rather, the overall plan is to be adjusted regularly as circumstances change.
- Planning, if it is effective, forces the company to capitalise on opportunities as they occur.
- Planning includes staff considerations, such as employee development, benefits, salary and so on, so that the team can more willingly become involved.
- Planning goals and expectations must be clearly stated so that all members of the staff understand and perform accordingly.
- Planning is a means, not an end. When you are involved in the process, don't get so preoccupied with the mechanics that you forget what your business is.
- Planning's underlying purpose is to get you from where you are to where you want to be.
- Planning is, for the most part, the responsibility of those who make the business decisions.

The diagram on page 51 depicts the key steps in the planning process. At the top of the diagram, in the first box, an analysis of major environmental issues is called for. The kinds of issue to be included in the analysis are:

- Economic trends
- Legislative and regulatory developments
- Industry trends
- Major concerns in the industry
- Competitive developments
- Product trends and cycles

Business Management Basics

- Staff issues: salaries, union issues, management development
- Financial trends
- Technological developments
- Company mission and current business plan.

The 'Do' in the boxes below Environment means that the MD and members of top management are concerned with the environmental analysis in creating/reviewing the mission statement, as well as in establishing the business plan and major company goals. Unit manager goals support company goals. Again, there is interaction among the various management levels.

The next step, the second box from the left, calls for key decisions that establish the level of priority various actions will be given. These decisions are communicated down through the organisation (the 'Do' in the boxes means that directives are given to lower management levels). Specific goals are then generated at the unit manager level and sent up for management review at the top levels of the company (the 'Review' function shown in the boxes).

Action plans are then developed. There must be a concentration on specifics in the action plans and on means to measure results. Broad action plans are reviewed at top management level, then directed to lower levels where unit action plans are generated before being sent back up for integration and review.

Implementation follows. In the implementation step, consideration must be given to time frames, budget integration, and the communication plan. Full implementation means that every employee in the company understands what he or she has to do to help the company make the plan.

After implementation, the next important step is the quarterly review. Implementation is only significant if the results of the action plans are known and analysed. Adjustments to action plans are made, as appropriate, each quarter.

The last step in the process is really the first step in the next annual planning cycle. After an updated review of the environment, the steps follow in the same sequence.

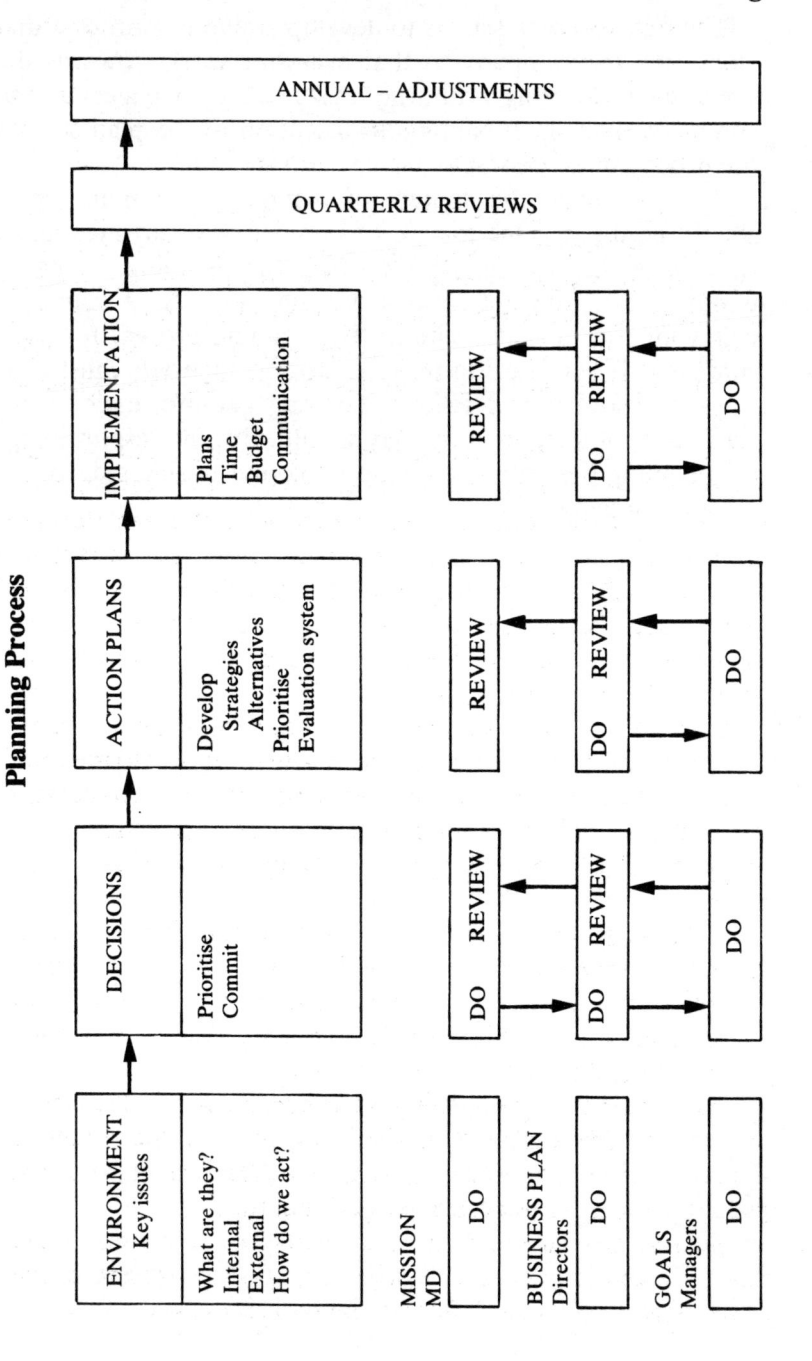

Planning

Planning Process

ENVIRONMENT
Key issues
- What are they?
- Internal
- External
- How do we act?

DECISIONS
- Prioritise
- Commit

ACTION PLANS
- Develop Strategies
- Alternatives
- Prioritise
- Evaluation system

IMPLEMENTATION
- Plans
- Time
- Budget
- Communication

QUARTERLY REVIEWS

ANNUAL – ADJUSTMENTS

MISSION
MD — DO

BUSINESS PLAN
Directors — DO → DO REVIEW → DO REVIEW → REVIEW

GOALS
Managers — DO → DO REVIEW → DO REVIEW → REVIEW

Business Management Basics

The fundamental issue is to develop a planning process that works for the company so that everyone works towards the same goal. Starting with the MD, every manager in the company must show continuous attention to the plan so that the process stays on track.

Before leaving the subject of planning, one more point should be made. One mistake a number of companies make is to have the 'wrong' people doing the planning. Planning is not a staff function. It is a line function. As a manager, it is your job to participate in the planning process for your company. If you want to make decisions, then you must plan ways to make better decisions. You may get information from staff units; in fact, you probably should. But the responsibility for planning lies with those who make the business decisions for the company.

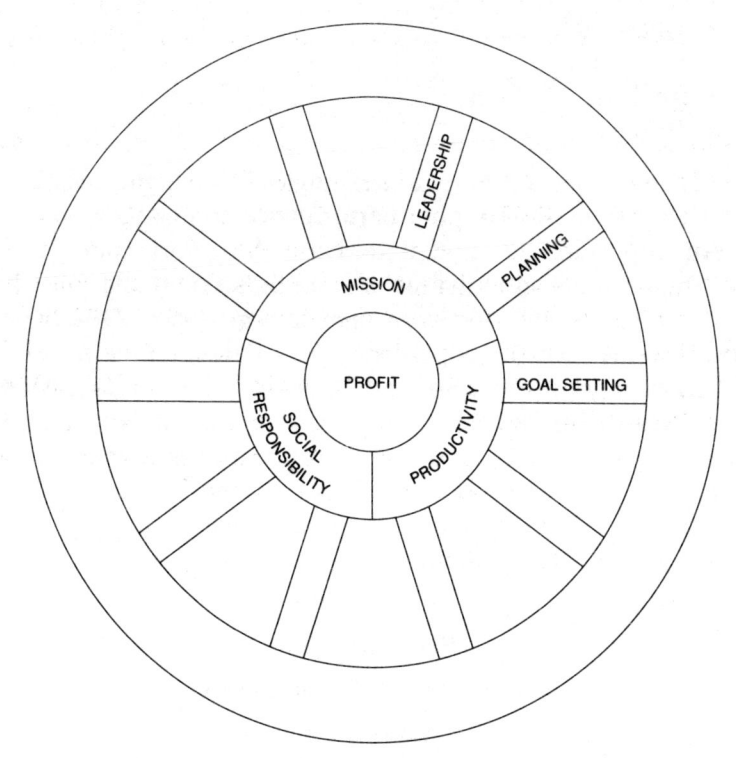

Chapter 9
Goal-Setting

(An organisational skill)

Effective goal-setting is fundamental to company performance. Goal-setting can be accomplished with relative ease, provided that goals are interactively established and concentrated on. There should be dialogue between manager and staff concerning what the goals should be so that the goals relate directly to the jobs being performed. One firm calls for a 'Smart' approach

Business Management Basics

to goal-setting. The goals established must be:

- Specific
- Measurable
- Actionable
- Realistic
- Timely.[1]

Otherwise, goal-setting is a meaningless ritual, the results of which are time wasted, poor performance and frustration.

An important question underlying the smart approach is how many goals an individual should be accountable for. The best answer is *not one more than is reasonable*. Otherwise, you run the risk of jeopardising all of them. *Five to six* is probably a good range to start. Less may not stretch. More may overwhelm. Whatever the 'reasonable' number of goals turns out to be, it is important to remember that goal-setting is an event. The process of acting to reach goals will be concluded, and the act of setting new goals will recur. The cycle runs something like this:

Prepare goals
↓
Conduct quarterly reviews
↓
Conduct annual performance reviews
↓
Prepare new goals

The process begins with the manager and subordinate jointly establishing goals. Progress towards these goals is reviewed quarterly or regularly. Regular progress reviews provide the opportunity to adjust goals if appropriate and for feedback from manager to subordinate. The annual performance review will contain no surprises for the subordinate if regular progress reviews have occurred.

Some additional considerations are also necessary for effective goal-setting.

- **Simplicity** of form is key. Limit the form to one page so that *you* use it. Limiting the number of pages will help to force clarity and improve mutual understanding. You and your subordinate should understand each other without too many words and figures written on a piece of paper.

Goal-Setting

- **Agreement** between the person setting the goals and the 'boss' is critical. (Notice that the person setting the goals is not the boss.) Agreement requires dialogue to ensure that a mutually acceptable level of accomplishment is sought.
- **Review periods** become self-analyses on progress and must occur at regular intervals. Putting it bluntly, regular reviews are a must.
- **Annual performance reviews** are another must (at least annually, and more frequently if that is your company's policy). Concerning the performance review, a few points are worth noting.
  — First, don't mistake activity for accomplishment. Make sure that progress has occurred.
  — Second, remember that poor performance is also a reflection on the manager who fails to use the quarterly reviews as opportunities to redirect the subordinate's activities.
  — Third, make sure the goals are attainable, clear, and that they aim for *improved* performance.
  — Fourth, ask yourself if you could achieve what you are asking your subordinate(s) to achieve.
- **Personal goals** are fun to include with business goals. A personal goal, such as losing weight or becoming active in a charity, helps to humanise the relationship between the manager and the subordinate. Accomplishing personal goals also improves the individual's self-esteem.
- **Changing goals** is perfectly acceptable if the circumstances warrant change and if the manager and the subordinate agree that the change is for the better.
- **Lower-level goals** (at lower levels in the organisation), must be more specific, have narrower limits and relate directly to the work performed.
- **Responsibility/Authority/Accountability** go hand in hand with goal-setting. If you cannot delegate or accept these three, don't bother to set goals.

Business Management Basics

As a manager, you should look at the goals of those two organisational levels below. Let the staff at the lower level know that you are following their progress. Of course, handle this arrangement carefully and with the concurrence of their boss (your subordinate).

On the following page is a goal-setting form. It has all you need on one page. If you don't like it, find or develop another. But make sure that your form is clear – not too much information, not too little.

If you want to perform well, you must manage your staff so that they perform well. Your effectiveness at setting goals (your own *and* those of your staff) is the propellant that gets you where you want to be in terms of performance level. Within the framework of your company, goal-setting is an organisational propellant. Setting goals will be successful if:

- Driven by purpose
- Clearly communicated
- Mutually agreed.

Notes

[1] *The Growth Management Process Workbook*, 1983, Growth Management Centre Inc, Palos Verdes, California, USA.

Goal-Setting

Goals

GOALS	ACTIVITIES	REVIEW PERIODS
		— — — — — — — —
		— — — — — — — —
		— — — — — — — —
		— — — — — — — —
		— — — — — — — —

PERSONAL
(OPTIONAL)

		— — — — — — — —

PREPARED BY   REVIEWED BY   REVIEWS & DATES

DATE   DATE

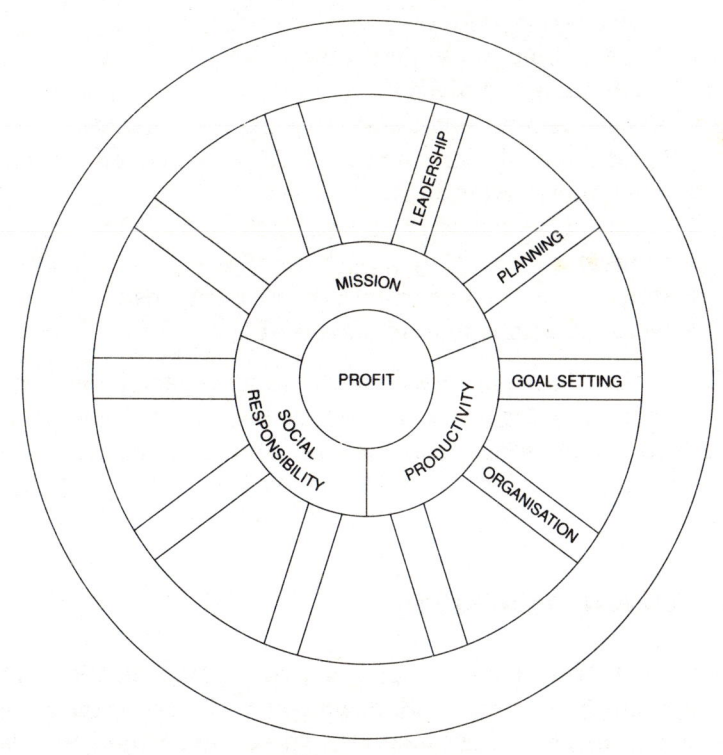

Chapter 10
Organisational Structure

(A management skill)

Creating and maintaining proper organisation is a management skill. The organisational structure is a means to 'running the company'. It serves as a delivery system. Think for a moment about your company and what the formal organisation is designed to do. Here are the primary functions of the organisation for your company – as a matter of fact, for any

Business Management Basics

company. The organisation is created to:

- Carry out the mission of your company.
- Deliver your product or service to the market.
- Allow people to use their capabilities.
- Facilitate productivity.
- Assign responsibility, authority and accountability.
- Minimise confusion and conflict among the various functional interrelationships.
- Facilitate communication among the various units in your company.
- Build pride of ownership in the work process.
- Help the company to make a profit.

While these functions are common to all organisations, there is no common organisational design that fits all companies. Let's consider some examples of different structures that are appropriate for the kind of business the company is in.

Functional organisation

This kind of structure emphasises the major functions performed in the company. Management and staff resources are clustered around these functions. An example would be a data processing company that has three major divisions (designating the major functions): Computer Operations, Systems and Programming, and Hardware. These divisions, of course, report to a managing director. Labour and management expertise are assigned according to function.

Geographic organisation

This structure is appropriate for companies that have operations distributed over a large geographic area. Management and staff support functions are distributed into geographic centres. A large national retailing company comes to mind. The geographic area covered is the United Kingdom. The entire area is divided into regions with senior line managers and staff who are

Organisational Structure

responsible for the individual retail shops in cities assigned to each region. The regions report to company headquarters.

Product organisation

Management and staff resources are assigned to major product lines in this structure. A car manufacturer comes to mind here. The major divisions are cars, trucks and financing (in this instance, financing refers to the service offered to buyers to lend them money so they can make the purchase; a financing service/product).

Customer segment organisation

This kind of company is organised around the major market segments (customer segments) that are served. An example would be a bank with major divisions established according to basic customer groups: consumer banking, personal trust, corporate trust, national corporate banking, international corporate banking and so on. The structure recognises the customer segments because the financial requirements of the various groups are distinctive and, in some cases, dramatically different. Management and staff specialise according to the segment served.

Process organisation

Major divisions in this structure recognise the key stages in a process. An example is a large farming company that has these divisions: crop production (growing), harvesting, packaging and distribution. Getting the product from the ground to the market involves passing through major steps, each of which requires different management and labour skills. The structure accommodates the process and the skill differences.

As you can see, different organisational structures serve different purposes. What can be very good for one company can be entirely inappropriate for another. The job of top management is to blend purpose, function and resource (management and

Business Management Basics

staff) in the best way to deliver the service or product to the market in the most effective manner. The organisation *serves* the operating needs of the company. Operating here refers broadly to manufacturing, marketing, distribution and so on.

There are other structures that come into and go out of vogue. A few years ago, for example, the matrix organisation was quite popular. In this structure, management and staff are grouped according to professional speciality and then allocated to operating units on a dotted line basis. An example is a centralised research group whose time and efforts are allocated to major product divisions. Individual members of the research group are assigned to the individual product divisions (dotted line reporting) for support but continue to be accountable to the research group management (solid line reporting). But this kind of structure can create some serious internal difficulties. The individual research group member effectively has two masters – the research manager and the product manager. There can be battles over which manager's judgement prevails when disputes arise. Accounting for the cost of the research resource can be confusing when an individual or unit in the research group serves more than one product division. And what if the product division does not like the quality of the research resource? The matrix organisation in many instances caused more problems than it solved and has been abandoned by many companies in the recent past.

Another structure that looks like a conventional organisation, but does not function well, is the top-down structure:

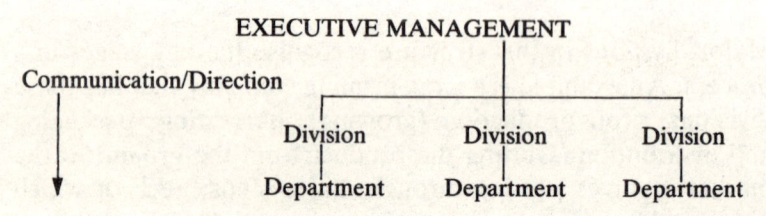

```
                    EXECUTIVE MANAGEMENT
                             |
Communication/Direction      |
   |            ┌────────────┼────────────┐
   |         Division     Division     Division
   |            |            |            |
   ▼         Department   Department   Department
```

In this kind of company, management makes all decisions unilaterally and passes them down through the organisation.

Organisational Structure

This may work in a small entrepreneurial company, but it will not work well in larger organisations. The issues are too many and too complex for one or two at the top to make all the decisions.

Although the organisation chart below looks the same as that of the top-down structure, the nature of the management process is significantly different.

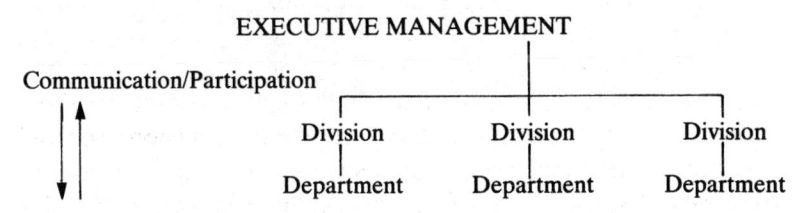

```
                    EXECUTIVE MANAGEMENT
                             |
Communication/Participation  |
      ↑↓        ┌────────────┼────────────┐
                Division    Division    Division
                   |            |            |
                Department  Department  Department
```

Note that communication is up and down. Participation means that lower levels of management make input into decisions taken at the higher level. This allows the top managers to take advantage of the knowledge of their subordinate managers, improving the prospects for sound decisions at each organisational level. Yet some additional characteristics need to be present for this structure to function well:

1. Within each unit (department, division), someone must be in charge – the boss – and ultimately responsible for decisions and unit performance.
2. Responsibility must be appropriately assigned to each unit (department or division) according to the function that unit performs. Marketing, for example, must not be assigned the responsibility for quality control in the manufacturing units.
3. Authority to make the necessary decisions must be granted with the assignment of responsibility.
4. Accountability for the decisions made must be tied to the authority to make decisions.

A discussion of organisation also calls to mind the committee. There are really only two kinds of committee: the helpful and the harmful.

- *Helpful* committees provide advice and counsel to line managers and are a vehicle for communication in the company (assuming, of course, that several units are represented on the committee).
- *Harmful* committees are assigned or assume decision-making responsibility. One of the early warning signals that a committee is becoming harmful is a request from the committee for support staff. With a staff, the committee begins to think of itself as a line unit and will soon begin to interfere with the line managers in the company.

If you serve on a committee or create one, make sure the committee members understand that they are to advise, to use their own resources from their respective units as needed, and to disband when their advice has been rendered.

The organisational structure of a unit or group, a committee or a company must be viewed as a means to getting the job done. An effective organisation consists of parts that function harmoniously and purposefully. As applied to the company overall, it delivers the product or service to the market efficiently and at a profit. Regardless of the size of the group you manage, your organisation must have the attributes described above in order to serve you and your company well.

Succession planning

As long as we are dealing with the subject of organisation, let's consider a few thoughts concerning succession planning. A mixed bag of observations can be made about succession planning:

- It is critical to an orderly evolution of the organisation over time.
- It can be done simply.
- It must be done regularly.

However,

- It is sometimes ignored.
- It is frequently made complicated, even esoteric.

Organisational Structure

- It can lose purpose if the succession planners become so involved in the process that they lose sight of the objective.

The succession planning form on page 66 shows how the process can be performed for a relatively large number of units – simply and even on one page. The example shows different managers (each box) and four organisational levels. Jones, the group manager, is at the top, and Johnson, manager of district B, is at the lowest level shown. Under each box are three crosses. Beside each is a space for the name of the first candidate to take over if the incumbent manager leaves, the second candidate, and the third choice if the first two do not work out. Three candidates, identified in order of preference, will be adequate most of the time. We should also point out that the candidates can be drawn from other units within the company, or even from other companies if appropriate.

Look at the box for Sam Smith, region 1. The first two spaces are blank; only the third X has a name beside it. This means that the only individual known to Smith is not the best candidate for Smith's job. Other candidates should be identified. Whatever the reasons are for this situation, Smith must make it his business to identify potential candidates within a reasonable period. He may have to call upon the human resources (personnel) department to help him look for candidates within the company or identify some candidates on the outside.

You should have a succession plan for your unit. Use a form like the one shown here to develop succession candidates for the managers/supervisors that report to you. Also, if some of your workers have highly specialised skills, you may want to consider succession planning for them. Keep your succession planning process simple and the paperwork to a minimum, and update your plan regularly. When changes in staff do occur, you will be prepared.

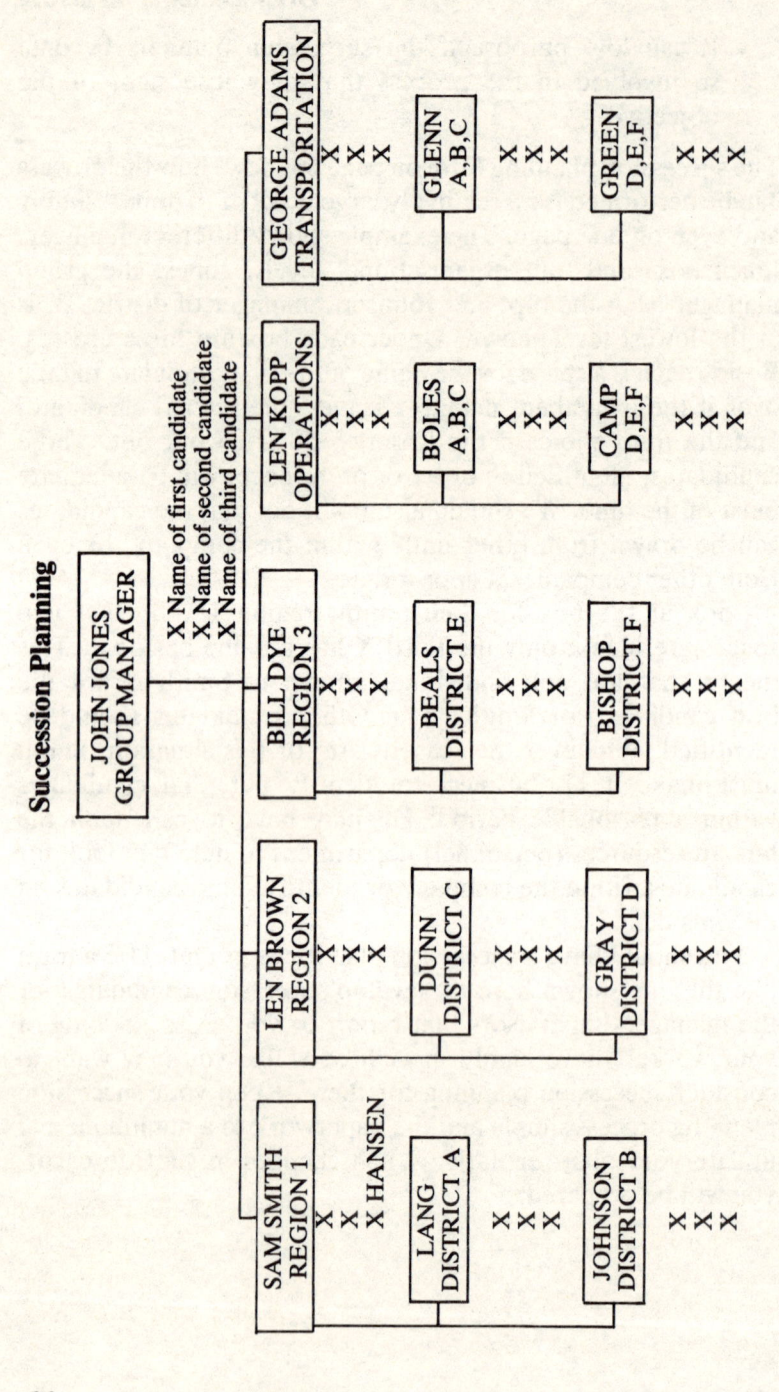

Succession Planning

- **JOHN JONES — GROUP MANAGER**
  - X Name of first candidate
  - X Name of second candidate
  - X Name of third candidate

SAM SMITH — REGION 1
- X
- X
- X HANSEN

LANG — DISTRICT A
- X
- X
- X

JOHNSON — DISTRICT B
- X
- X
- X

LEN BROWN — REGION 2
- X
- X
- X

DUNN — DISTRICT C
- X
- X
- X

GRAY — DISTRICT D
- X
- X
- X

BILL DYE — REGION 3
- X
- X
- X

BEALS — DISTRICT E
- X
- X
- X

BISHOP — DISTRICT F
- X
- X
- X

LEN KOPP — OPERATIONS
- X
- X
- X

BOLES — A,B,C
- X
- X
- X

CAMP — D,E,F
- X
- X
- X

GEORGE ADAMS — TRANSPORTATION
- X
- X
- X

GLENN — A,B,C
- X
- X
- X

GREEN — D,E,F
- X
- X
- X

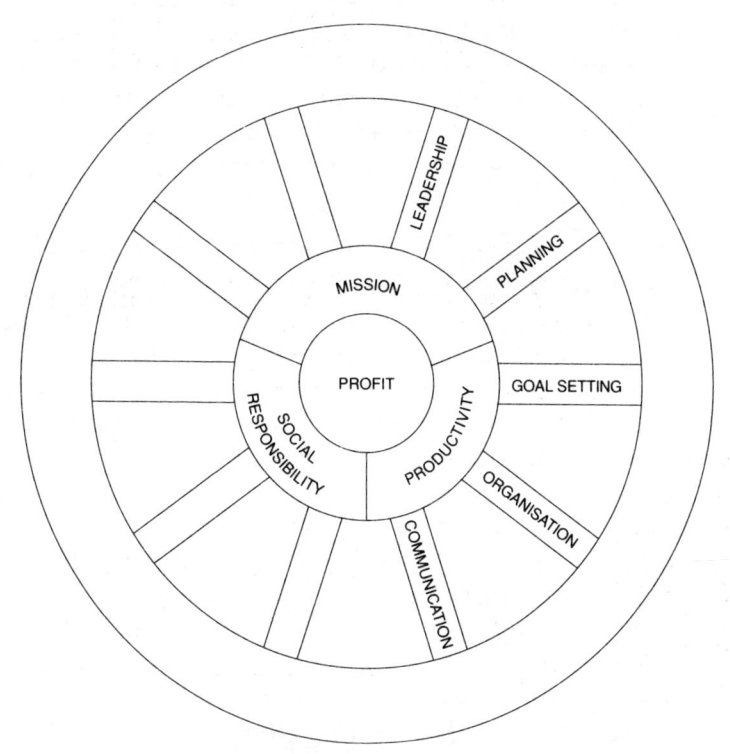

Chapter 11
Communication

(An organisational skill)

Communication plays such a vital role in business that its value is difficult to overstate. Whether it be an advertising message, a performance appraisal given by a boss to a subordinate, or a mission statement, communication occurs only when there is a transfer of information between people that produces a *common* understanding. Business, as is the case with any

Business Management Basics

social or political system, is dependent upon a common understanding. Consider your company: can you imagine the disorder that would result from individual employees running in different directions? The company would collapse. Your role as manager is equally dependent upon communication. For you to be effective, your employees must have a common understanding of their jobs, of their relationships with each other, and of your expectations for them. Let's review briefly the components of the communication process.

- **What**. Communication is a *two-way* flow of information. The two-way characteristic calls for both saying something and listening to something. You have no doubt heard the quote from the hard-headed manager: 'Don't confuse me with facts! I've made up my mind!' You may even know a manager who behaves this way. The same attitude may be more subtly manifested when suggestions by subordinates to do something different consistently fall on deaf ears. On the other hand, a good manager exchanges. Better communication, like better management, is participative.
- **Why**. Communication takes place for one of three purposes – to inform, to direct or to request. Unclear communication will misinform and misdirect: everybody suffers. If the wrong request is made or the request is unclear, the chances of getting the desired results are weak. Clear communication precedes obtaining the desired result.
- **How**. The most common methods are, of course, oral and written communication. But there are some important complements to these two forms. Your tone of voice carries a message equal to, or greater than, the words you speak. Your actions express the values that govern your behaviour: one *act* (of temper or patience, of panic or calm under pressure, of defensiveness or self-confidence) is worth more than a thousand words. And it should not surprise you to know that communication occurs without a single word: when the boss closes the door, communication occurs.

These characteristics are straightforward. Understanding them

Communication

is easy. You have already learned how to make them yours. You have been communicating for a long time. You are no doubt pretty good at it. Let's try a little test to see how good your communication is. Following are several statements. Write one of three descriptions in the space provided after each statement. The descriptions are:

1. Always
2. Some of the time
3. Haven't thought about it.

Here are the statements:

- I recognise that effective communication is hard work.
- I know what needs to be said before I speak or write.
- I think about my audience – who they are, what their level of interest is likely to be, and what their level of understanding is.
- I choose the right words, for the subject and the audience.
- I try to be interesting.
- I am aware of the environment (office or social setting, open or closed door, morale, boss preoccupied, etc) when I communicate.
- I look for feedback.
- I listen with the same level of interest I want given to me.
- I seek common understanding.

Now give each of your answers the appropriate value:

Always = 1
Some of the time = 2
Don't think about it = 3

If your total score is less than 10, you are a superb communicator. A score between 10 and 12 means that you are probably pretty good – you really should think about these statements most of the time. A score that exceeds 12 suggests that you run the risk of misdirecting, misinforming and/or requesting one thing and getting something else.

All this, of course, is simply to make the point that it is easier to think you are an effective communicator than to be one. In a study of several major companies, the managing directors

Business Management Basics

made the point this way: when asked which skill (from a list including technical, interpersonal, analytical and so on) was most important to success in management, the MDs responded with *communication* skill. This skill is critical to your success as a manager. If you write and speak well, you will get more out of your efforts to inform, direct and request. If you listen well, you will learn and accomplish more.

The same is true from a company perspective. Effective communication provides a common understanding. Work efforts are concentrated, purposeful and rewarding. Good communication benefits everybody.

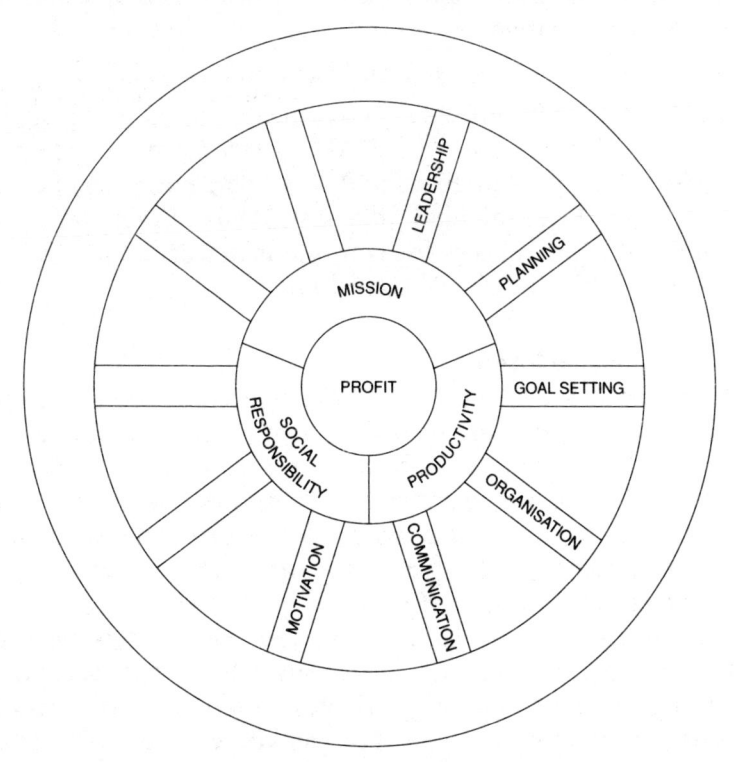

Chapter 12
Motivation

(An organisational skill)

One of the best stories about motivation is the one about the factory workers at a steel manufacturing plant:

> The night shift wrote their night's production on the floor when the shift ended. The day shift saw the production figure and set about to improve on it. At the end of their shift, they

Business Management Basics

scratched out the night shift's number and wrote their *better* number on the floor. The night shift responded, and the competition carried on with the obvious consequences for production output.

The story may not be literally true, but the message is on target. Motivation affects performance. You easily recognise that a motivated employee accomplishes more. A group of motivated people (a department or a company) accomplishes more. Therefore, the view your staff holds of their work has significant consequences for you, the manager. So let's spend some time thinking about motivation.

The Hawthorne Effect

Elton Mayo, between 1927 and 1932, undertook one of the first modern studies of work behaviour as it relates to productivity. The study took place with worker groups at the Western Electric Hawthorne plant near Chicago. Looking for ways to explain levels of productivity, Mayo's experiments actually demonstrated the effects of motivation. The results became known as the *Hawthorne Effect*.

Mayo used several variables to test their effects on productivity. Music, painting, increased lighting and decreased lighting were among the variables tested. But the results were consistently the same. Productivity went up. The most influential variable, not even considered for the original tests, was that of the workers' reactions to being tested, their reactions to the *attention* given to them. The environmental variables faded in importance when compared with the human variables – interest and attention – given to the workers at the Hawthorne plant. The human variable raised the level of motivation and, consequently, the level of productivity.

The significant point here is that *human beings react to other human beings*. Your staff, be it two or two hundred, will react to you. The interest you take in your staff, and the attention you pay them, will have more to do with their level of motivation than anything else. Level of motivation has more to do with the level of accomplishment than anything else. Understanding your staff, what makes them 'turn on' or

Motivation

'turn off' to the work process is key to your being able to get things done through them. Let's consider how some expert views apply to your influence on the level of motivation among your staff.

Maslow

In 1954, Abraham H Maslow described the hierarchy of needs in *Motivation and Personality*. Consider the hierarchy in terms of the work situation.

Physiological

The physiological needs are for food, sex, drink and sleep. If these needs are not satisfied, the employee will not be motivated. For example, if the salary earned is insufficient to provide for the physiological needs, the employee's first concern will be to find ways to earn more. This may take the form of moonlighting, of numerous job changes, or of theft from the company. While you cannot, and indeed should not, know the personal circumstances of every employee, you can be aware of whether or not the salary structure generally seems adequate for the majority of your staff (you'll know because they will let you know). If it is not, there is little value in trying to raise their performance level markedly. You had better consider whether your salary scale has to be adjusted. This may mean that a formal salary survey has to be undertaken. If you cannot authorise it, you should request it. There is not a great deal you can do at this level of need. Being aware of the general situation with your staff and making higher levels of management aware when common sense dictates is about all that you can do.

Safety

Stability, freedom from fear, structure and order are the safety needs. At this level, your influence starts to be more noticeable. An orderly work environment, an attitude of purpose and commitment on your part, a reasonable show of tolerance rather than throwing your weight about are the ways you influence the level of motivation associated with the safety needs.

Business Management Basics

Feelings of belonging and love
The presence of family and friends satisfies this need. In the business context, a small amount of effort in showing the individual or group that what they do is needed and valued by the company goes a long way. Employees need to know that they are part of the team, that their jobs are important to the company's overall ability to function.

Esteem
Self-confidence, respect for others, usefulness and competence are the needs at this level of the hierarchy. Showing appreciation for a job well done is key. Take an employee to lunch, or call a staff meeting to single out an employee who has done something well. Show some recognition, and you will build esteem among the members of your staff. Greater self-respect raises the prospects for respecting others, which must exist if people are to function as a team.

Self-actualisation
Growth and development of potential is the last and highest level of need in the hierarchy. This is the area of greatest influence for you as manager. If an employee consistently performs well and wants to do more, give the employee a chance to do more. It will be necessary for you to help your employee to assess potential. It will motivate your employee if he or she believes that you will help to develop that employee's potential, even if it means that you may lose the employee to another department in the company.

Better managers in better companies deal effectively with the hierarchy of needs that Maslow pointed out. Understanding the hierarchy and applying the concepts to your management situation can only improve your relationship with your staff and your company.

Motivation

McGregor

In *The Human Side of Enterprise*, 1960, Douglas McGregor discusses how people are viewed (not necessarily how they are) in his descriptions of Theory X and Theory Y. Applied to your attitude as manager, the theories go as follows:

In Theory X, the manager believes that the average employee:

- Inherently dislikes work
- Must be punished and controlled, directed towards work objectives
- Prefers to be told what to do.

A manager who takes this view is more likely to be autocratic. There is little room for acknowledging the basic worth of the individual employee and little hope that the hierarchy of needs will be met.

In Theory Y, on the other hand, the manager believes that the average employee:

- Finds effort at work as natural as effort at play
- Wills self-control, works towards objectives, is committed
- Enjoys the rewards of achievement, which themselves regenerate commitment
- Has the capacity to exercise the imagination – is creative in finding solutions to problems, is broad-minded rather than narrow-minded.

The manager who takes the Theory Y view is more likely to be participative, seeking the contribution that individuals make to improve the work process. This kind of manager is more likely to be a team builder and will have a more highly motivated group of people as a result.

On any given day, of course, people differ. At various points in time, the attributes of both theories will apply to all managers. The significant point here is those attributes that apply to each manager *over time*. If you take the fundamental view that people have needs *and* abilities, you will find that they are motivated by organisational objectives and will be able to achieve them.

Business Management Basics

Common sense
Let's put what you do as a manager in terms of the dictates of common sense.

Need: People want to know what is expected of them.
Action: Tell them.
Need: People want to achieve.
Action: Give them goals and a chance.
Need: People want to be noticed.
Action. Pay attention to them.
Need: People want to believe.
Action. Give them a mission.
Need: People want to be appreciated.
Action: Say thanks.
Need: People want to care.
Action: Care, and *they* will.

There are a few additional points that can help you to create and maintain a high level of motivation among your staff. They are basic and can be applied naturally.

- A *sincere* 'thanks' is worth any number of motivational speeches.
- A reprimand is warranted, when warranted. Don't overuse it, but don't be afraid to use it.
- A compliment is a standard, as well as an expression of appreciation. With most people, saying 'well done' will result in more opportunities to say 'well done'.
- A motivated employee is terrific. Build a team of motivated employees.
- A winning team consists of individual winners.

Winning companies are made up of motivated people. They desire to do well, are rewarded for doing well, and will continue to do well. After all, it's fun to win.

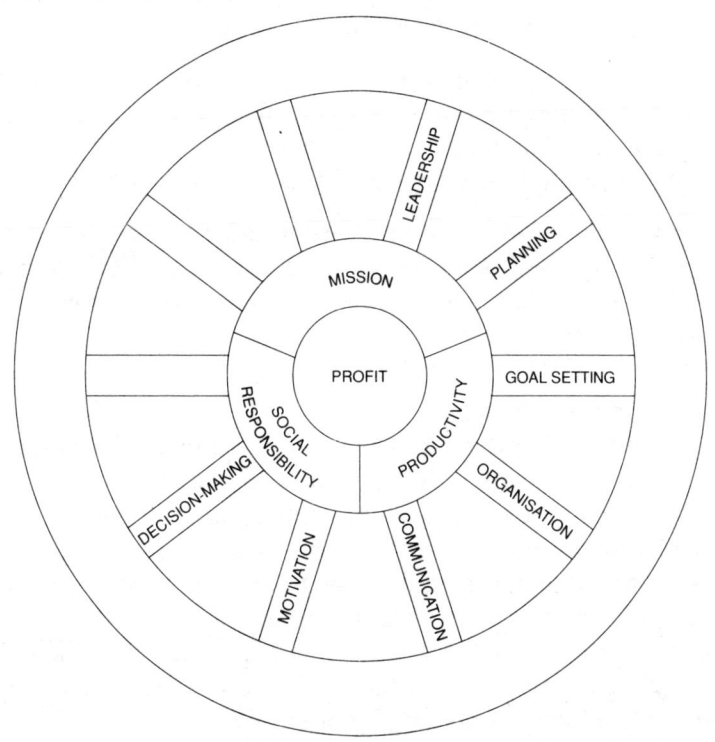

Chapter 13
Decision-Making

(A management skill)

Decision-making is obviously a management responsibility but, after several years of observing the process in various companies, it is clear that decision-making is a responsibility that many managers have difficulty carrying out. A decision, of course, is a choice selected from alternatives. One alternative is not to make a decision. But because there are undesirable

Business Management Basics

as well as desirable alternatives, the choice the decision-maker finally makes can be good or bad. The good decisions are generally based upon informed choice and, as Chester Barnard, points out, are decisions sometimes not made:

> The fine art of executive decision consists in not deciding questions that are not now pertinent, in not deciding prematurely, in not making decisions that cannot be made effective, and in not making decisions that others should make.[1]

It does seem, however, that decision-making is less than a fine art when handled in an inappropriate manner. Let's consider some examples of inappropriate methods (and enjoy a little humour while we're at it).

The committee decision
This kind of decision occurs when an individual cannot, or is afraid to, decide. The committee decision syndicates the personal risk, leaving no one individual accountable. The decision is subject to change at the next committee meeting. The committee decision is easy to communicate, however, because each member takes away his or her version of what the committee decision was. If challenged, the individual can simply explain that the committee view prevailed over the right view, and there was nothing he or she could do about it.

The participative decision
This is a more contemporary label for the committee decision, but don't be fooled. The process of participative input has been confused with the process of making a decision.

The impulsive decision
This kind of decision occurs when the press of events does not allow for rational consideration. Or it may be a matter of personal style.

The analytical decision
This decision is still in process – has not yet been made because further analysis is needed.

The *right* decision
This is the decision that everybody claims to have made.

The *wrong* decision
This decision is one that everybody attributes to everybody else.

It is important to emphasise that decision-making is, in the final analysis, an individual matter. The processes that lead to a decision vary according to circumstances and should, if possible, involve input from others. Some decisions do allow for input and collection of information leading up to the point of decision. Other decisions call for a high degree of intuition and judgement. In the strongest companies, with the strongest managers, some*one* makes the decision, some*one* is accountable.

Not all decisions will be good ones regardless of the quality of information available or the strength of personal judgement. In fact, the person responsible for making decisions will make some bad ones. If no bad decisions are made, it is likely that not enough decisions are being made. As Edward John Phelps put it, 'The man who makes no mistakes does not usually make anything.'[2] Better managers make many decisions and accept responsibility for the consequences, good or bad. But bad decisions serve to broaden the reservoir of understanding from which every decision is drawn. You should not fear making a bad decision as much as you fear making a series of bad decisions.

The fundamental process associated with decision-making goes as follows:

Pre-decision
This stage calls for the manager to recognise the opportunity, problem or need to decide something. The better manager has a system of some kind to produce the recognition. For example, staying in touch with the staff two organisational levels below you can help to determine which problems need solving, which decisions are clearly understood, and how your decisions are

Business Management Basics

being interpreted and applied. The pre-decision stage also calls for determination of who should make the decision; that person must then (within the time dictated by the particular circumstances):

- Gather information
- Develop alternatives
- Analyse alternatives
- Choose the best alternative
- Make the decision.

Although this sequence is ideal, frequently time does not permit thoroughness in each step. Judgement and intuition are called on in the absence of time and information.

Implementation
Once the decision has been made, it has to be implemented. Weak managers are much more capable of drawing conclusions than they are of making decisions and implementing them.

Post-decision
After implementing your decision, you must evaluate it. If you have made a good decision, hold on to it. On the other hand, make another if the first decision was a bad one. Generally, it is not too late to change your decision if the change is for the better. The mistake a number of managers make is staying with a bad decision as a result of personal pride or fear of admitting an error. Taking this position is a bad decision for you and your company. To be an effective decision-maker, understand what needs to be decided and who should make the decision. If it is your responsibility to decide, get as much information as time and circumstances allow. Then make a decision. Implement it, and learn from it.

Notes

[1] Cited in William R Tolbert, 'Executive Mind, Timely Action,' *Revision*, Vol 6, No 1 (Spring 1983), p 5.
[2] Edward John Phelps, *Speech*, 24 January, 1899.

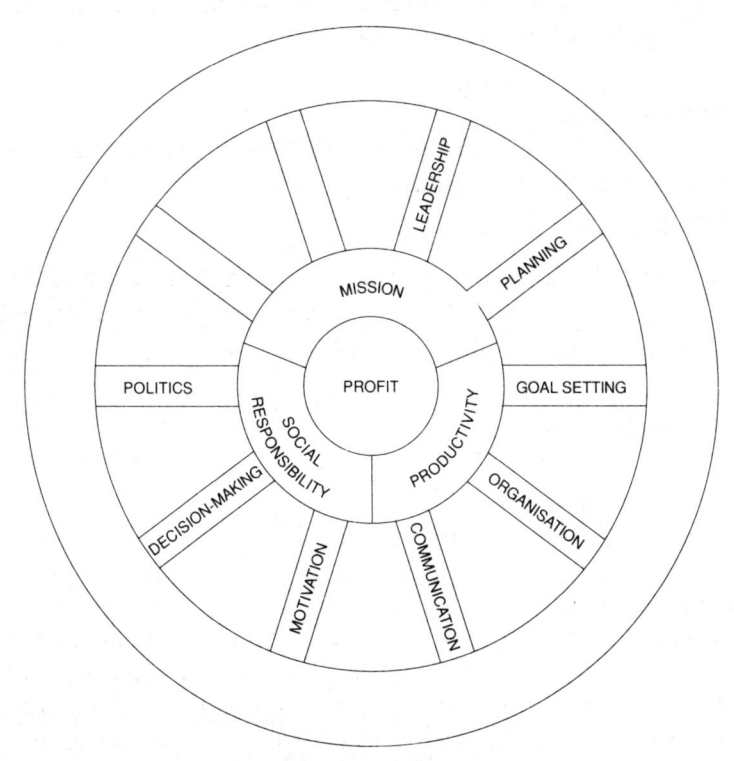

Chapter 14
Politics

(A management skill)

For some reason, there is a general aversion to an open discussion of corporate politics. It seems that a majority of managers claim not to 'play politics'. But the fact is that where two or more are gathered together in the name of the corporation, there will also be corporate politics. Politics are pragmatic. They are necessary to get the job done. They can

Business Management Basics

be wholesome or unwholesome, beneficial or harmful. But they must be recognised and dealt with.

It is best to begin a discussion of corporate politics with some of the ground rules of the game:

Peers are competitors
The truth is that your peers are competing for the boss's attention, for company resources, and to be first at the right time and place.

Play fairly
This rule is apparently easily forgotten because it is frequently forgotten. If you are good at what you do, you can play fairly and win. Remember that, over time, people generally deserve what they get.

Know the players
Understand the strengths and weaknesses of your team and those of your competitors, both in terms of professional abilities and of position within the company.

Know the stakes
Understand that you can win more responsibility, more salary, more opportunity. You can also lose your job, if not your career.

Now that you are familiar with the most important ground rules, you need some equipment to play the game:

Sponsorship
You need a sponsor in the organisation. Someone you can trust, who trusts you and has confidence in what you can do. Someone who can coach reliably. Someone who ranks highly enough in the company to be able to help you to take advantage of opportunities, grow and distinguish yourself. Someone who can help to cushion you as you make mistakes.

Commitment
If you can't hang in, don't play. While most of the world sleeps, you must lie awake thinking about what you have done and how you could have done it better, what you *can* do better than most, what you *will* do better than most.

Poise
Whether giving a presentation to the board of directors, having a casual conversation or debating an issue, you must maintain poise. Probably the best way is to be yourself, but stay calm if you tend to let go easily. Remember, it's a short step across the line from the dramatic to the melodramatic.

Mind
You must have an active and capable mind, keen and able to foresee the possibilities of what can be – good and bad.

Each player has to use individual skills when playing the game, but following are a few techniques that may prove to be helpful:

Concentrate on corporate purpose
If your efforts are directed largely towards personal gain, you incur great risks. Remember that the best blend comes from a merging of personal and corporate goals.

Be honest
Sometimes it may seem more expeditious to be otherwise. But when truth and error are on the field of battle, truth wins out over time.

Let there be no surprises
Your foremost obligation is to be frank with your management. Make sure that you keep them informed. Most of the time, they will help you more as a result.

Form strategic alliances
The chances are that you cannot do everything yourself. You

Business Management Basics

sacrifice something of self by allying with others. But the collective alliance is better off than its individual members would have been on their own. These alliances may take you across organisational boundaries and are generally formed 'after hours'. Make sure, however, that strategic alliances are used for the benefit of the company: otherwise, they may be purged and take you with them. An example of a strategic alliance is a task force with individual members from several different departments within the company. Friendships are formed and the task force members 'help each other out' both within and outside the task force efforts. The help may take the form of keeping each other informed privately about what is happening in various units, or developing a new idea or concept to present to management, or alerting others when the boss is about to crackdown.

Use people's time well
Take no more time than is necessary with your boss and your staff. Learn to recognise the distinction between exposure and over-exposure.

Be friends with secretaries
Secretaries wield enormous power. They are highly influential. They know a lot about what's going on. They talk to the boss more than anyone else in the company. If you are friendly, they can help. If not, they can be formidable adversaries.

Do more than asked
Think, anticipate, worry, and work harder than most.

Be right
Most of the time.

Think
Replay discussions in your mind to learn from them. Evaluate situations, before and after. Know yourself. Think about what needs to be done and what you can do to get it done. Then think some more.

Politics

If you have not done so already, you will find times when you are in the middle – between what you believe to be right and what your boss believes to be right, between opposing issues, between two executives that are in opposition to each other. There is no prescription that tells you how to deal with the dilemma created by these and similar tensions within the company. You have to assess and decide upon alternative courses of action. And hope you're right.

> A few years ago, a manager in charge of administrative support for a large company was caught in a dilemma. Two directors were known to be competing for the top job and, therefore, always willing to criticise each other (on a behind the back basis). Let's call them executive A and executive B. The manager was known and close to both executives. The manager reported to executive A, who also had the personnel department reporting directly to him.
>
> The manager learned that one of the senior officers who reported to executive B was using his company expense account for entertainment in violation of company policy. The violation was not blatant, so there was a good possibility that it would go unnoticed. But if discovered, both executives would certainly find out that the manager had known about the violation of policy.

Put yourself in the position of the manager. What would you do? If you tell your boss, executive A, he will create a fuss over it with the MD to discredit executive B. Executive B will know that you spilled the beans and be angry with you for not having told him in confidence so that the matter could be quietly resolved. If you follow this course of action, your boss (executive A) may find out and never trust you again. If you say nothing, the risk is that the matter will surface and both executives will never trust you again. What would you do under these circumstances?

> The manager chose the following course of action. He first went in confidence to executive B. He told executive B what the senior officer in his unit was doing with his expense account. He also told executive B that he would have to

raise the matter with executive A, his boss. He then went to executive A, told him about the expense account violation and that he had brought the matter to the attention of executive B, because the violation occurred in his area of responsibility.

Executive B was able to take steps to remedy the situation quickly. Executive A reported the matter to the MD, but also knew and reported that the situation had been corrected. The manager survived because he acted in the best interests of both executives and the company. The course he chose may not have worked under a different set of circumstances, but it did work under the existing circumstances.

In the final analysis, you can only do your best. But, guided by the principles of integrity and a good 'people sense', your chances are pretty good. If you want to play the corporate game, you must accept the reality of corporate politics. They exist in varying degrees in every company. Understand them and deal with them.

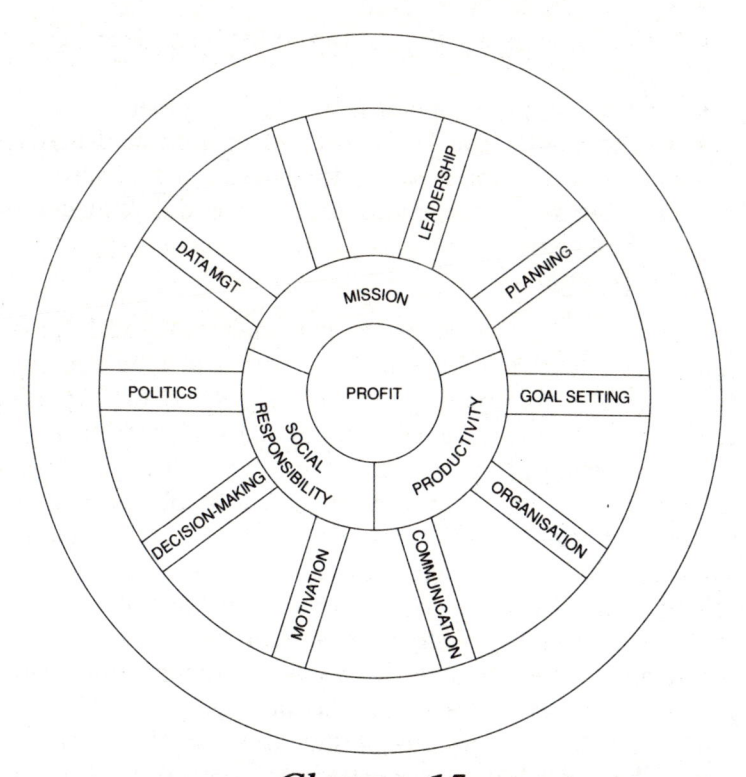

Chapter 15
Data Management

(An organisational skill)

Some managers are managed by data. The better managers manage data. The best managers transform data into information because they recognise that *information is power*. The simple fact is that proper management of data is critical at all levels of the company. Good data management allows the manager to:

Business Management Basics

- Make better decisions because they are informed decisions
- Make decisions more easily
- Make distinctive presentations to the boss, peers, and the staff
- Ensure that performance goals are being met
- 'Control' after the fact – that is, an informed manager knows more about what to expect and reviews data resulting from operations to confirm that expectations are being met
- Sleep better.

An important characteristic of good managers is that they know more about their areas of responsibility than anyone else. From masses of data, they home in on areas of pertinent information: key financial ratios, variances from plan, turnover statistics and so on. Knowing the pertinent information offers you several pragmatic benefits. You can more easily obtain company resources because you are informed and make intelligent requests. When challenged by an internal rival, you can defend yourself because you know what is happening in your area of responsibility. Also, you can react quickly to questions or criticisms from the media, analysts and others. Information gives you the power to act and react intelligently.

In order to stay on top of the area for which you are responsible, you must be satisfied that the proper financial, operating, and quality controls are in place. You must be able to ask relevant questions of your staff and understand the accuracy of their answers. You must be able to provide intelligent answers to questions asked.

The 'lift question' comes to mind here. This is the situation in which you are in the same lift as your MD or another top executive in your company. The MD asks you a question. You have 15 seconds to reply. If you scramble to answer, the MD will know – and may remember. With good information, you can respond well to any senior executive. A flood of words is a sure sign that you really don't know what you are talking about. And in a situation like this, silence is deafening.

One executive we know is responsible for several regions, large numbers of people and facilities, and about 40 per cent

Data Management

of the company's profits. Everywhere he goes, he takes a small briefcase. In that briefcase are key operating indicators – financial ratios, market share trends, productivity measures, staff turnover trends, etc. This year's data compared to previous years'. Actual compared to plan and projected year end. He even has brief career profiles on key managers and 'high potential' staff members. When he has an extra few minutes (waiting for a train or plane or travelling to a meeting), he studies the data and extracts the pertinent information. He can answer virtually any question he's asked. He can make discussions with each regional management team relevant and informative. He can encourage staff at any level because he knows what is going on. He is one of the best leaders/managers we have come across. He is the most informed and *powerful* executive (under the MD) in his company. His company rivals are afraid to take him on. He enjoys an excellent rapport with members of the board, media representatives and industry counterparts. He wins.

Regardless of the size and scope of your unit, you should be well informed. Determine what you need to know and then arm yourself with this knowledge and information to succeed.

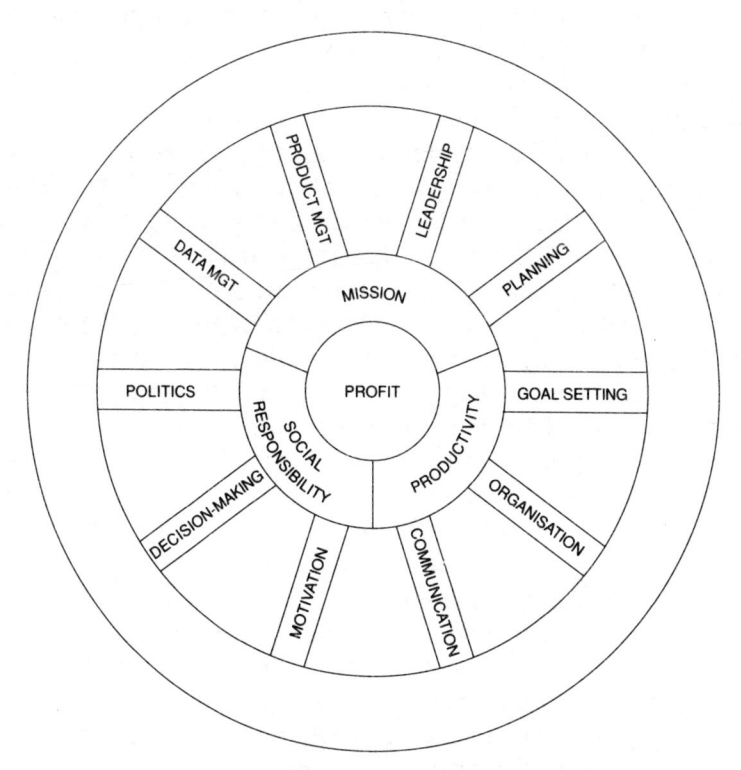

Chapter 16
Product Management

(A management skill)

Product management is treated here as a skill. If you disagree and believe this function in a company is another professional skill (like finance or personnel), that's all right. But this management activity has evolved to the point that it has most of the attributes of other management skills. In the future, product management will play an increasingly important role

Business Management Basics

in many industries. Therefore, we believe that you should be familiar with the function.

Two important reasons support our view that product management will play a greater role in the years ahead. First, all companies, whether they sell products or services, have to operate in a world that is becoming increasingly complex. Specialisation is increasingly necessary in interfacing with the market-place. For example, large accountancy firms perform audits which specialise (a fundamental product management characteristic) by industry. They have tax departments, executive recruiting departments and consulting departments, which also specialise by industry. For some time now, these firms have moved away from general auditing. Procter & Gamble, along with many other product-orientated companies, have excelled using the product manager concept. Financial service institutions are in the initial stages of application of the concept.

Second, product management is a people orientated management concept. The product manager is a 'leader' for a product or service, but the leader works with a team of people. The process itself is enriching to members of the team and decentralises creativity and initiative. Employees' 'ownership' (personal involvement) is more widespread within the company. Also, because the product manager is a focal point for a product or service, staff members know where to go when they have questions, suggestions or complaints.

Product manager's scope

The product manager is the *champion* of the product or service within the company and has a vested interest in its success. The scope of concern is broad. Let's consider some of the areas a product manager has to worry about and find answers to some key questions.

Planning
Does the product or service fit into the overall company plan and help the company to reach its goals?

Product Management

Profitability
Does the product or service make enough profit to meet the company's profit targets?

Legislation/Regulation
Are we aware of change that will affect our product? Do we have a system to keep abreast of legislative and regulatory developments (making contacts at industry conferences and other ways to communicate with people outside the company, industry newsletters, and so on)?

Statistics
Do we have the right data to make informed decisions and stay informed as trends change?

Competition
Do we have a system for tracking the competition? Do we actually interact with the competition (eat at a competitor's restaurant, apply for a loan at a competitor's bank)?

Training
Is our training relevant, and available to the right people?

Advertising
Do we work closely with our company's advertising agency to give input concerning the major message we want to get across to the market-place?

Service quality
Do we test our product or service using such means as professional shoppers, customer surveys and so on? What internal measures do we employ to monitor quality?

Software/Hardware
Do we have a system that will allow us to stay current with what our competitors are offering in the market-place?

Business Management Basics

Product enhancement/Improvement
What improvements are needed? Are they being developed?

Staffing
What level of staffing is needed to support the product in the field? What new skills are required to keep the staff up to speed?

These and many more areas fall within the product manager's range of concern. The product manager has to see that these things get done: that is, manage the process (not do everything), which frequently calls for assistance from other units in the company. For example, if there is a salary problem (the staff assigned to a given product area complains that competitors pay more for the same job), the product manager has to go to the personnel department to request a survey, letting the professionals develop the necessary information and make a recommendation. If the results show that the staff complaint is valid, the product manager must decide on the appropriate course of action: do nothing or obtain the necessary approvals to remedy the complaint. Like other unit managers, the product manager has to draw on other resources within the company when the need arises.

Product management structure

There are essentially two structures that a company can adopt for product management. These represent opposite ends of the spectrum to make the point. In fact, the structure actually adopted in most companies has characteristics of both.

Fully staffed
Under this structure, necessary resources are assigned directly to the product manager. However, the risk here is that the company as a whole is disadvantaged because resources are duplicated in the different product management units. For example, every product manager needs market research

Product Management

support. With four product managers, there could be market research staff assigned to each, as opposed to having one centralised function that supports the four managers. This duplication seems easier to avoid than it actually is – a strong product manager can mount convincing arguments for direct control of the resource needed to support the function.

Task force

Under this structure, representatives from corporate resource groups (centralised support functions, such as market research) are assigned to the product manager on an 'as needed' basis. For example, a specific individual from each corporate resource group would be designated to serve on the task force: a representative from finance to assist in analysis, from personnel to help develop training programmes, from legal to deal with copyright and patent concerns, and so on. The disadvantages of the matrixed organisation (discussed under Organisation) can surface under the task force structure if not properly monitored. With care, however, the task force can be efficient and expeditious.

As mentioned above, most companies use a combination of the two to enjoy the advantages of both. For the purpose of making a distinction, we favour the task force structure as generally being the most effective. A model of a product management task force is given below.

Product Manager

Operations	Market research
Legal	Advertising
Government relations	Public relations
Finance	Facilities
Marketing collateral	Personnel
Data processing	Audit
Hardware	Sales
Software	

Market-Place Representation*

*Someone from the line units that interface with the market-place.

Business Management Basics

Use of the task force structure allows members from various organisational units to help build the product, plan the implementation and watch it perform. As a result, the members usually '*buy in*', making the product manager's job much easier on a continuing basis. Subsequent interaction with the resource groups for assistance is easier. Individuals from those groups are already familiar with the product, if indeed they did not help build it. The product manager is more likely to encounter a receptive attitude.

Organisational placement

Placement of the product manager in the organisation is critical to success of the function. Under the fully staffed structure, the product manager is probably a line manager.

On the other hand, if the product manager is not positioned as a line function with appropriate authority, the product management approach is more difficult to implement. Using the financial services industry as an example, the product manager for cash dispensers (automated teller machines or ATMs) may not manage the physical locations, the employees that service the machines, or the employees who interact directly with the customers using the machines. In this case, the product manager must have line management support in order to be effective (line managers responsible for those servicing the machines and interacting with customers). One way to increase the probability of line management support is to position the product manager as a senior officer reporting directly to the executive in charge of the line managers whose support is needed. An example follows:

```
                        Director
                  Retail Banking Division
     ┌──────────────────┬──────────────────┐
Senior Executive   Senior Executive   Senior Executive
ATM Product            Region 1           Region 2
  Manager           Branch Offices     Branch Offices
                        ATMs                ATMs
```

While this reporting relationship for the product manager will not eliminate all the tension, it helps to communicate to the regional managers that the director in charge views the function as significant.

Personal skills

When the product management function is treated seriously, the product manager has a high profile in the company. Because the product manager is a champion of the product in the company, good product performance means that the manager is considered a highly performing individual. The reverse is true if the product does not perform. The personal skills of a product manager are key to the performance of the product in the market-place. A weak spirit, a reluctance to be criticised, insensitivity to needs of the market-place are certain to prove themselves fatal to the life of the product. The effective product manager is:

- A good communicator (which includes good listening)
- Highly interactive with people, and pleasantly so
- A self-starter
- Analytical
- At least in part, a visionary
- Politically effective within the company
- A negotiator
- Experienced with the product or service managed.

Without these attributes, the product, the manager and the company will suffer. The selection of the individual to serve as a product manager is a major consideration in whether or not the function will succeed.

Introducing a new product

Good managers are constantly on the lookout for opportunities to develop and introduce new products or services. A model to help you think about this is the Product Wheel on page 98. Following the example of a financial services institution shown on the Product Wheel, try to build a wheel for your company, product area, or unit. Start with the market-place (consider

Business Management Basics

opportunities from the viewpoint of potential customers). Dream up ideas for new products or services you could offer. Let your imagination run, at least for a while. Then select some of the ideas that seem to make the most sense. Ask a few questions about each idea that survives:

- Does the market-place need it?
- Is the competition offering it, or something similar?
- Do we have the necessary resources within our company to develop and implement the product or service?
- Can we make a profit with it?
- Does it fit into our statement of mission?

If the answers are positive, ask yourself a few more questions:

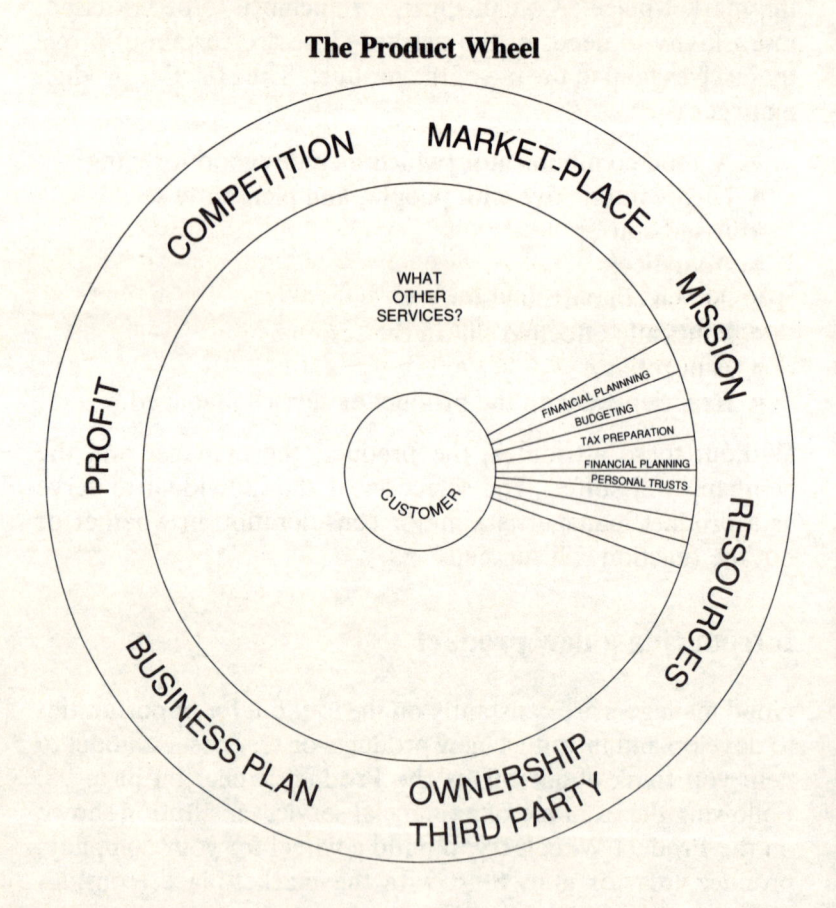

The Product Wheel

(Diagram: concentric circles labeled around the outer ring with COMPETITION, MARKET-PLACE, MISSION, RESOURCES, OWNERSHIP THIRD PARTY, BUSINESS PLAN, PROFIT. Inner circle contains CUSTOMER with wedges labeled FINANCIAL PLANNING, BUDGETING, TAX PREPARATION, FINANCIAL PLANNING, PERSONAL TRUSTS, and WHAT OTHER SERVICES?)

98

Product Management

- Can I find a sponsor (someone high enough in the company and with sufficient authority to acquire resources and commitment)?
- What interest level among top management can be obtained?
- Will a task force structure work? If not, which structure will?
- Should we build it or have it built?

If the answers to these questions are positive, start the process. One of the most interesting challenges a company faces is that of developing a product and getting it to the market-place. The idea for a new product seems to get started in one of two ways. Either management recognises an opportunity for a new product and picks an employee to be product manager (a person to champion the idea), or an employee approaches management with an idea. In either case, the steps below are to be followed.

First, before wasting a lot of time, energy and money when considering the introduction of a new product, find someone in the company (the sponsor) who has the clout to make it happen – provided, of course, that the idea makes sense. If a member of top management has the idea, the sponsor requirement is met. This point is illustrated in the following graph.

Starting a New Product

Corporate title

```
10
 |\
 | \       Good
 |  \
 |   \
 |    \
 | Poor \
 |       \
 0────────10
```

Management interest

Business Management Basics

If the product is proposed by a low-ranking title and there is little interest from management, it will appear in the shaded area. If the title is high-ranking or if the idea is received with enthusiasm by the management, it will appear in the white area and will probably succeed. The probable success of a new idea is calculated as a function of corporate title and top management interest:

Lowest:	Low-ranking title	0
	Low management interest	0
	Probable success =	0
Highest:	High title	10
	Great interest	10
	Probable success =	20
Break-even:	Title	5
	Interest	5
	50/50 chance =	10

Second, have the sponsor coordinate the assignment of task force members through his peers in the company. This means the director of manufacturing talks directly to the sales director.

Third, arrange a time and place for regular meetings of the task force. This gives added seriousness to the effort.

Fourth, discipline the process. Keep minutes (and circulate them through the sponsor to the right people – the sponsor's peers – in the company). Assign responsibilities to task force members and hold them accountable. Establish a reasonable time-table for tasks and adhere to the schedule.

Fifth, assuming the product makes sense and is developed, involve the task force members in the development of the implementation plan. This way the need for line and support resources is scheduled in accordance with the time-table established for implementation. For example, introduction of the new product should not clash with a major sales campaign arranged for an existing product.

Sixth, reward the task force members when the project is completed. Make it fun – dinner, T-shirts, badges – and visible in terms of top management attention. A personal letter of appreciation from the managing director to the task force members does a lot.

Product Management

Even if you do not have direct responsibility for product development, you can think about how products or services are managed within your company. Who is accountable for them. Who is making sure they are right for your company's mission and the market-place served. After all, the chances are that your competitors are thinking about the matter. Careful thought and effectively structured product management can bring substantial success to your company's performance in the market-place.

Organisational Resources

Every company employs people, delivery systems, capital and the other resources referred to in the Management Wheel to carry out business. Management's job is to use these resources to create and deliver something of value to sell at a profit in the market-place.

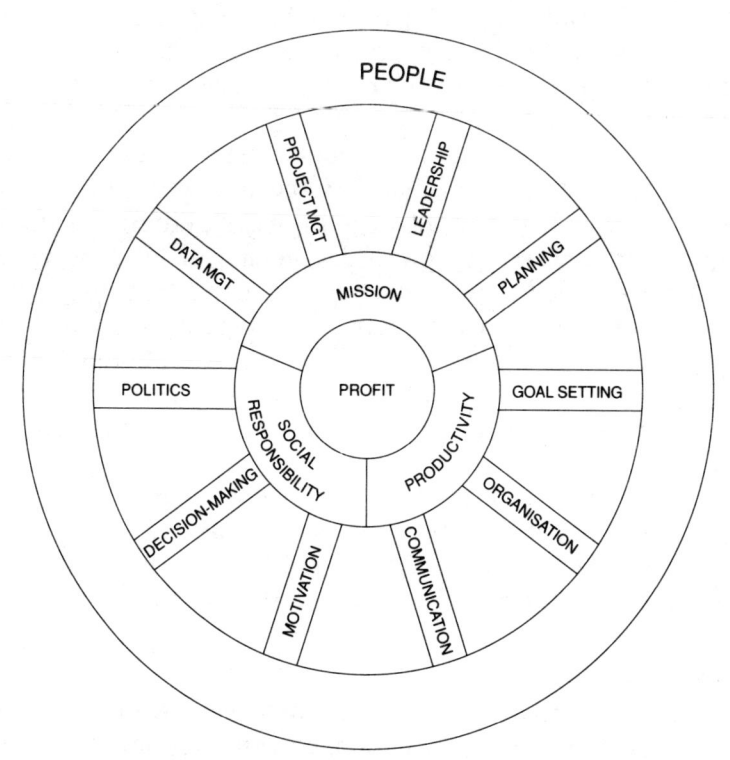

Chapter 17
People

(A resource)

Throughout our discussion, we have referred to people in various contexts. One business convention is to classify people as a resource. Although appropriate from an analytical perspective, this classification can strip away the *humanity* of people. A renowned historian once observed that every enterprise (be it science, art or politics) is, in the final analysis, a

Business Management Basics

human enterprise. The quality of the enterprise reflects the quality of the people involved in it. This is also the case in business. Companies don't perform. People perform. Inherent in the constitution of every company is the assumption that it is of people, by people and for people. Management is through people.

Looked at as a resource, people come to the company in varying states of readiness. Some are more green than others. People have varying degrees of skill, differing learning capabilities and, on any given day, higher or lower levels of motivation. What they do have in common is that they work for the same company but people are different. They work for different reasons and perform at different levels. For individual reasons, some will stay with the company longer than others. People may be considered a resource, but they are clearly the most diverse and dynamic resource the company employs.

As a manager, your job is to employ this resource effectively in your company. Essentially, the best managers are the most effective 'match-makers'. Let's consider what match-making means. Five fundamental matches need to be made.

Task with skill

The greatest service done to the employee and the company is to match the task to be done with the skill to do it. The reverse is also true. Too little skill results in defective output, lack of productivity, discouragement and, in many cases, forced termination of employment. Too much skill results in defective output, lack of productivity, boredom and, in many cases, voluntary resignation. In either situation – too little or too much – everybody (customer, shareholder, employee, manager, company) loses. The strength of the good manager lies in matching the basic range of skill with basic job requirements. Ideally, there is some room for the employee to learn and improve, but not too much. It is your job as manager to find the right balance. Obviously, there is no precise formula for making this match. That's what managers have to work out. And to complicate matters further, there are usually supervisors between managers and workers. Managers,

People

through matching supervisory requirements and skills, have to ensure that supervisors are making the right matches at the worker level.

Training with need
Although people should have a basic sense of how their job fits into the company framework, they need to be trained to do specifically what the job calls for. The role of training is not to provide general enlightenment or to teach everybody about everything. Training must be in response to need. Train the worker to perform specific tasks. Train the supervisor to supervise a specific series of tasks. Train the manager to manage a specific process.

Accomplishment with reward
Levels of accomplishment differ. Rewards must differ correspondingly. The course of least resistance too often is to expect more, but reward in a uniform way so that everyone comes out about the same. Recognise and reward performance. A low level of performance that is tolerated becomes deadwood. A high level of performance that is unrecognised goes away, perhaps to a competitor.

Responsibility with accountability
Hold people accountable for the responsibilities you give them. If you assign or delegate responsibility, give the employee the latitude to do the job and hold him or her accountable for the consequences of their actions. Otherwise, the risk is that the performance may become irresponsible.

Desire with opportunity
Not every employee who performs well at one level wants more responsibility. But some do. People who have learned how to do their jobs, have demonstrated that they perform well, and have expressed the desire to do more, must be given the opportunity to handle more responsibility. Pushing them too fast, of course, is not good. Neither is leaving them too long. But if they can do more and want to do more, see that they get the opportunity,

Business Management Basics

even if that means transfer to another unit in the company. With the right matches in these instances in particular, everybody (customer, shareholder, employee, manager, company) wins.

Looking at people as a resource is a conceptual exercise, but it is not to be confused with management practice. Viewing people as a resource when analysing the cost of labour or quantity needed to get the work done is entirely appropriate. However, management is employing people effectively. Be a better match-maker and you'll be a better manager.

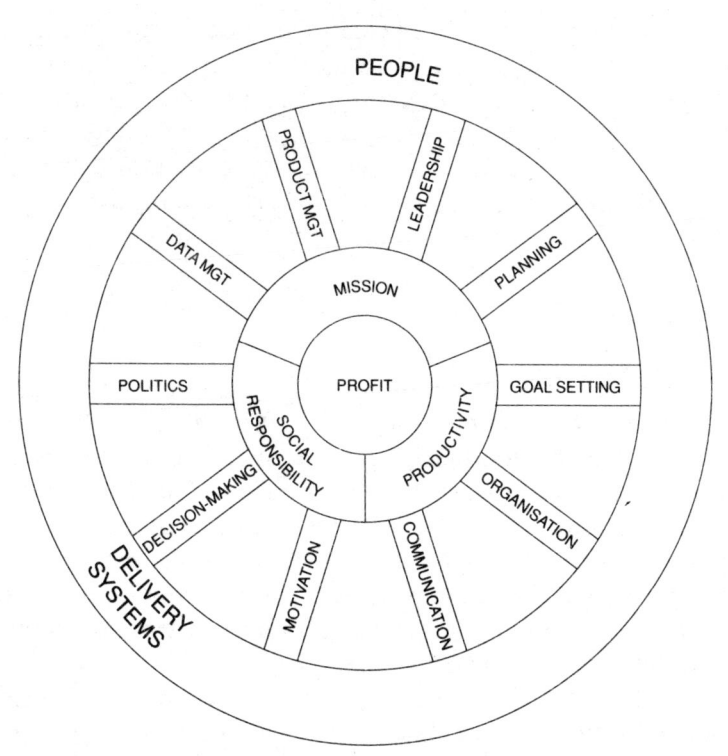

Chapter 18
Delivery Systems

Although delivery systems can be complex and expensive, they perform a simple function: getting your product or service from you to your customer. Depending upon the nature of the business, the alternatives available can be many or few. There is, of course, no single delivery system that is appropriate to all companies, but three areas of consideration should be associated with all delivery systems.

Business Management Basics

Convenience

As mentioned earlier, convenience is one of the factors influencing the potential buyer's buy-decision. Therefore, one characteristic of your company's delivery system(s) must be that, relative to the competition, it is easy for the buyer to get access to your product or service. If your competitors hold the advantage, you must consider and evaluate alternative delivery systems.

Efficiency

It is critically important for you to know the unit cost of delivery for your product or service. You have to have your own costs delineated before you can measure your company against industry norms or the estimated unit cost of delivery for your competitors. The cost of delivery, of course, has an effect upon the price of your product or service in the market. You may be all right, or you may need to consider automation. You may need to consider another type of delivery system altogether. Your delivery system needs to be efficient.

As is the case with other concerns, however, the emphasis upon efficiency can be taken to an extreme. For example, some security analysts have consistently criticised several service industries for too much investment in, and high costs associated with, *bricks and mortar*. More should be done electronically, argue the analysts, with less dependence upon physical outlets. One service industry MD of a large company responded this way: 'It's true that we can have too much tied up in bricks and mortar. We can have too many outlets in a given geographical area. Where we do, we have to close some. But it's also important that we don't overreact and throw the baby out with the bath water. Look at the basics. We are an organisation of people providing services to customers, who also happen to be people. We need a place for these two people (us and them) to meet. We can't make the process electronic if the customer wants to talk face to face. We need to be careful about bricks and mortar, but we must also be careful not to get carried down a path that leads us to maximum efficiency and no customers.'

Human element

Remember that very few delivery systems do not call for a place where two human beings (seller and buyer) interact. The most powerful, or weakest, link in the delivery chain is the human link. A motivated, capable employee *delivers*.

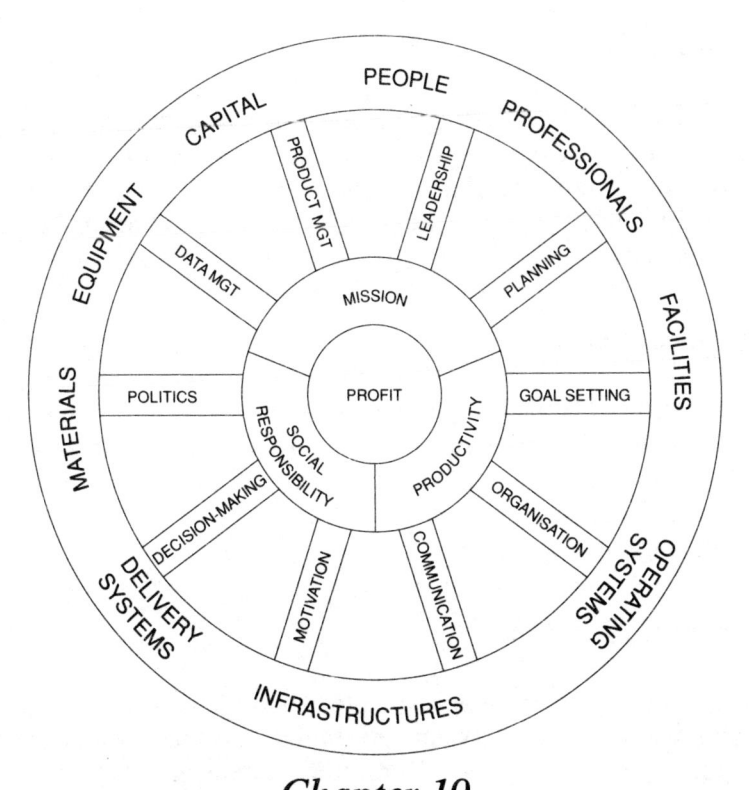

Chapter 19
Other Resources

We'll make a few summary observations about the remaining resources in the Management Wheel. The important points to remember are:
- Resources in themselves are an expense. When acquired, they are entered on the profit and loss account as an expense.
- Resources must be employed to produce revenue that

exceeds the expense of acquiring and employing them. Then the company makes a profit.

Capital

About capital, you should know that the easiest time to acquire money is when you don't need it. Have alternative sources in case one or more of your investors or lenders closes the door when you need capital. And plan for your capital needs before they occur.

Professionals

Professionals (solicitors, accountants, human resource specialists, public relations experts, and so on) are a *means* to an end. Don't have too many of them, and make sure their roles are clear. Solicitors, for example, are there to give legal advice, not make business decisions.

Operating systems

Good operating systems expedite delivery of what you sell, minimise the time between the initial customer contact and completion of the sale. Operating systems must have the controls to ensure quality and preserve the integrity of your enterprise. Your people must be able to use them, not be used by them.

Infrastructures

Know which infrastructures are relevant to your company's operation. For example, before you construct the building, make sure the work force you need is there, that they can get to work easily, that you can get supplies brought in efficiently, and that you can get your product out efficiently.

Materials

About materials, don't get more than you need. Also, remember that you usually get what you pay for.

Equipment

State-of-the-art equipment is good, but not always the best alternative. Be sure the equipment is functional and that it functions. A penny saved could cost you a fortune.

Unless you occupy a senior management position in your company, you will probably use resources provided by the company. But it's not too soon to start to think about the concepts referred to here; you may even consider learning something about them. Concentrate your energies first, though, on the concepts in the Management Wheel that are most immediate to your current management role.

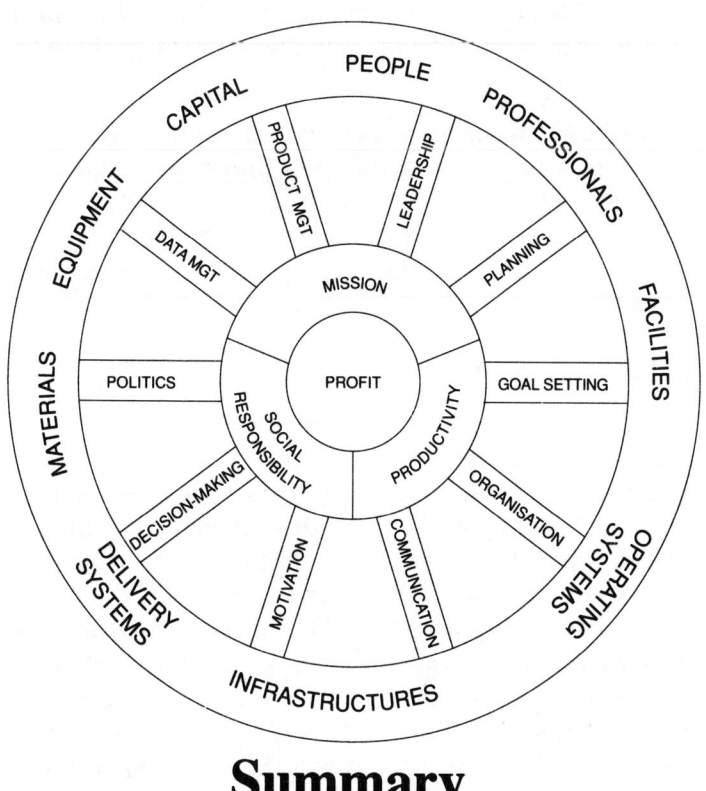

Summary

That's management. You have all the basics, every key concept you need to be a manager. How you use the basics will make you a good manager, a better manager, or in fact the best manager in your company.

After a seminar, someone asked, 'What is the one part of the Management Wheel that is most crucial to my becoming the best manager I can be?' Unfortunately, the point was lost on that person. The point is that what you have to do depends on your specific circumstances. A particular situation may, for a time, call for emphasis on one task or skill or resource. But over time, all components of the Management Wheel come into play. The effective manager knows *when* to apply *what* and how to keep the wheel in balance. As you move across to, and up through, various management jobs in your company, keep three things in mind:

1. The basic management concepts do not change.
2. The specific requirements of various management positions do change.
3. You have to work out the appropriate application of the basics to your particular circumstances. (There are no magic answers.)

Francis Bacon said, 'A wise man will make more opportunities than he finds.'[1] Make yourself a better manager and you will find more opportunities. Determine what is expected of you as a manager and be determined to do more than is expected. Try to be the best, even though being the best at anything is reserved for only a few. One of the 'rules' of management is that if you don't care about being the best, nobody else will care whether or not you are. This is not literally true; but it is true that, in the area of personal and professional excellence, the ball is always in your court. While others must help, they can only react to your initiative, your desire to be the best that you can.

Every manager has the opportunity to excel. Some will. The best will earn their way up through the management ranks to occupy executive positions. Their experiences will teach them how to apply the basics to the most complex situations. Success does not come easily, but the best executives seem to perform their roles almost effortlessly:

> [The] 'Executive Mind' is the mental muscle that can operate as the fulcrum between a person's inner life and the outer world. It is the muscle that can transform habitual behaviour into inspired, creative, timely action; the muscle managing the play of attention at the interface of time and space. Just as bodily musculature provides a person leverage in space, so 'Executive Mind' provides leverage in time. Appropriate

Summary

financial leveraging for a family, an enterprise, or a nation are examples of this capacity. Just as the ultimate development of bodily leverage gives the great athlete (such as Nadia Comaneci at the 1976 Olympics) the appearance of almost effortless ease and spaciousness in the midst of the most complex movements, so the highest development of mental leverage gives the great executive the appearance of leisureliness amidst the most complex schedule, the most dire emergency, the most momentous decisions.[2]

Business needs better management. Better management comes from better managers. Better managers come from people who, like you, are called out from the 'easy routine', who are willing to do more than is expected. Your company will profit from your efforts. And so will you.

Notes

[1] Francis Bacon, *Essays*, 52, 'Of Ceremonies and Respects'.
[2] William R Tolbert, 'Executive Mind, Timely Action,' *Revision*, Vol 6, No 1 (Spring 1983), p 4.

Further Reading from Kogan Page

Essential Management Checklists, Jeffrey P Davidson, 1987
The First-Time Manager, M J Morris, 1988
A Handbook of Management Techniques, Michael Armstrong, 1988
How To Be an Even Better Manager, 3rd edition, Michael Armstrong, 1990
How To Communicate Effectively, Bert Decker, 1989*
How To Lead – So Others Follow Willingly, James L Lundy, 1990
How To Motivate People, Twyla Dell, 1989*
Making Your Business Competitive, David Jacobs and Alfred Homburger, 1990
The Practice of Successful Business Management, Kenneth Winckles, 1986
Profits from Improved Productivity, Fiona Halse and John Humphrey, 1987
Project Management: From Idea to Implementation, Marion E Haynes, 1990
Systematic Problem-Solving and Decision-Making, Sandy Pokras, 1990
Team Building, Robert B Maddux, 1988

* Also available on cassette.